THE NATURAL WORLD OF
NEEDLE FELTING

THE NATURAL WORLD OF
NEEDLE FELTING

Learn how to make more than 20 adorable animals

jacqui
small

FI OBERON

Photography by Brent Darby

First published in 2016 by Jacqui Small LLP
74-77 White Lion Street, London N1 9PF

ISBN: 978 1 910254 58 5

A catalogue record for this book is
available from the British Library.

2018 2017 2016
10 9 8 7 6 5 4 3 2 1

Printed in China

PUBLISHER Jacqui Small
SENIOR COMMISSIONING EDITOR Eszter Karpati
ART DIRECTOR Sarah Rock
SENIOR PROJECT EDITOR Zia Mattocks
PRODUCTION Maeve Healy

Contents

KEY
EASY •
MODERATE ••
CHALLENGING •••

Nature & Nurture

As a dilly-dallying eight-year-old, getting to school was a daily adventure. I'd dawdle through the fields of sheep and the dank valley, building up courage to run past the haunted mill before climbing the hill, up Vicarage Street with its weavers' cottages. Then I'd cut through the churchyard with its 99 yew trees and ancient gravestones and slip into the pretty Cotswold village school, just beating the bell.

Homeward, I might head down Tibbiwell Lane, where there were more weavers' cottages, a sluice bridge and a waterwheel feeding the pin mill, past the imposing American artist's house and past the lane to the old dye house. Eyes down, ignoring the path to Hangman's Cottage, I'd head back up into the light, through more fields of sheep, along the hilltop ridge and home.

When I started secondary school, I'd pile on the bus with the other children and chug past farms, past cottages where famous authors had lived, churchyards where famous artists were buried, and yet more mills. Mills converted into do-it-yourself stores, breweries, restaurants, hotels and bars. Past the mill where they made felt for the Queen's Beefeaters and into a school built with mill owners' money.

Proud of our rich cultural heritage, our literature, music, and arts and crafts, we happily went on outings to the houses of artists, both dead and living. We chanted poetry by famous local poets, their words immortalized in clay on the library wall:

What is this life if, full of care,
We have no time to stand and stare.
'Leisure', William Henry Davies (1871-1940)

The pin mill finally succumbed to the new economic reality in the early 1980s. I like to think that in its long history it might have made felting needles for the local felt trade.

It is not surprising to become a full-time designer and maker when your community is burgeoning with such creativity and your working life is buoyed up by their enthusiasm. I am eternally grateful that I come from a region where 'to make' is synonymous with 'to live'.

OPPOSITE I have a passion for pottery as well as textiles and surface texture. I leave throwing marks on my bowls and am drawn to impressing repeat patterns in my stamped porcelain needle pots. This love of rhythm is subtly replicated in the construction and process of felt making.

What is felt?

Wool felt is a non-woven material made of tightly entangled fibres of wool. There are two basic methods to create felt by hand: wet felting and dry felting, also known as needle felting.

Wool's ability to felt is born of its biology. Wool fibres are covered in microscopic scales, with each animal species having a defining scale pattern. The edge of each scale is raised where it overlaps the scale beneath. When fibres rub against each other, these scales will catch, causing fibres to tangle. This is the beginning of felting.

Wool manufacturing aims to avoid felting, so wool fibres are sometimes coated with an oil to help them glide over each other. They are carded (where clumps of raw wool are pulled apart and passed between drums covered with small pins) to remove debris, graded so fibres of equal lengths and fineness are grouped together, and repeatedly combed (passed over more drums) until the fibres sit parallel to each other. Finally, they are passed through a tube to achieve the recognizable lengths we refer to as slivers, tops, rovings or combed wool.

Felters would ideally interrupt the process when the wool has had the debris removed by carding but hasn't yet been repeatedly combed. Sometimes you can source batts of wool. This is when the wool fibres have been passed over the carding drum and lifted off as a sheet, rather than made into a roving (a long continuous cylinder of wool fibre). Batts often exhibit the more random fibre alignment that helps us felt faster.

Wet felting is the process of agitating wet wool until the scales on adjacent fibres catch. Soaking the fibres so they absorb water makes the scales more prominent and allows the fibres to move more freely. Heat and soap speed up the process. Protein fibres referred to as wool are sourced from sheep, goats, rabbits, llamas, alpacas and camels.

OPPOSITE Felt is an extraordinarily versatile medium that can be used to sculpt all kinds of shapes. These cute penguins are surprisingly easy to make (see page 88).

In the nineteenth century the burgeoning English felt trade gave rise to a new invention, a needle-felting machine. Hundreds of specially notched needles were repeatedly punched into a bed of carded wool. The needles are essentially the same today and are used in manufacturing and by hand-felters.

TOOLS, EQUIPMENT & TECHNIQUES

As with most crafts, progression sees you acquiring an array of tools and equipment. Initially, you need very little: wool fibre, needles and a felting block.

I would suggest a beginner purchases at least one size 36 needle and one size 38 needle, a felting block, approximately 100g (3½oz) each of medium and fine wool fibres. If pre-felt is available, buy 50 x 50cm (20 x 20in, or a fat quarter). Felt balls are great to start a new project. You will add more kit in time but it's refreshing to be able to get started in a very simple way.

Hand carder

Knitting needles

Felt needle pot

Tailor's chalk

Pliers

Needles in a domed felting block

Scalpel

Rotary cutter

Craft wire

Multiple-needle tool

Felting block

Selection of beads

Wool

Wool festivals offer a stunning array of fibres, and the displays are a joy to behold. Alternatively, an increasing number of retailers and online hobby stores offer an ever more sophisticated range of needle-felting supplies.

Wool fibre is sold with a variety of labelling methods. A wool producer might specify the species and breed, but with more than 100 sheep breeds, initially you need to judge wool fibre as being fine, medium or coarse by the way it looks and feels. Buy a small quantity to start with, to see how the wool performs and, with a bit of experimenting, you will gradually come to know your preferred breed. Note if anyone stocks batts or carded wool with randomly aligned fibres. Otherwise, you can use combed rovings and misalign the fibres between your fingers or by using a carding comb.

When wool is offered for sale online or by mail order, the seller may use a micron measurement to describe the wool quality. This refers to the diameter of each strand, or 'staple'. The smaller the micron measurement, the finer the wool.

THE ACORN TEST

To make anything in 3-D larger than an acorn, avoid fine wool. There is nothing more likely to put off a beginner than prodding fine wool with a fine needle just to make a felt ball. It's as tedious as asking a beginner to knit an Aran sweater using 1-ply wool and 2mm (US size 0) needles.

Fine wool is made up of many very thin strands. This gives the fibre its smooth, luxurious feel but also means that huge numbers of strands need to be felted together to achieve any significant volume. Now imagine that each strand is ten times as fat; when you scrunch those together, you create volume so much more quickly.

So, if you want to make something larger than an acorn, your choices are:
• Needle felt using medium or coarse wool (see numbers **3, 4, 7, 9, 13** opposite) and a size 36 needle.

• Start with some wool-based sheet material (see **1, 2, 5, 10–14** opposite; see also page 21).
• Start with a ball of yarn.
• Start with a wet-felted ball (home-made or commercially sourced).

FINE WOOL BREEDS

Fine wools (including cashmere, merino, alpaca and angora) have more densely spaced scales than coarser wools. They wet felt incredibly well, but this isn't as pertinent when needle felting. Try to visualize the volume you are aiming to create. Needle felters use fine wool fibres to add colour and detail to the surface of sculptures or to make finishing touches such as a bird's beak.

CURLY WOOL BREEDS (6)

Curly wool breeds (including Cotswold, Blue Leicester, Masham and Wensleydale) are used to create surface texture.

MEDIUM-GRADE WOOL BREEDS (7)

These include Moorit and Texel and are regularly used to wet felt balls and sheeting, and to needle felt the centre of something bigger than an acorn.

COARSE WOOL BREEDS (13)

These include Herdwick and Swaledale and are used to wet felt or needle felt large balls.

ALTERNATIVE FIBRES (8, 15, 16)

Larger suppliers stock soya-protein fibres, silk, camel, hemp, and so on. These might be used for ethical reasons or to add lustre and texture. If you are blending fibres, be aware that plant-based fibres and animal-based fibres take up dye differently. This variation can be used to add an interesting textural effect but could be disappointing if you are expecting a solid colour.

DYEING WOOL

Merino roving is available in a wide range of colours, but the choice is often limited in other grades of wool. This can be overcome by blending different qualities and colours of fibres together with hand carders or by dyeing wool fibres at home. I do both.

I have a pressure cooker and a slow-cook pot used exclusively for dyeing. I dye wool in batches of fine and medium grades. Some batches are dyed with commercial dyes, following the manufacturer's instructions, but whenever I can I use plant-based dyes. Plant- and animal-based materials react in different ways to dyes, but wool takes up colour relatively well.

Most plant dyes will fade quickly, a tendency we combat by mordanting the wool. While a mordant's primary purpose is to achieve colourfastness by permanently binding the dye to the material, it also brightens the final colour.

I regularly use one of two mordants: soya bean milk or alum (potassium aluminium sulphate). Some mordants are hazardous - as are some plants - so please check that what you are using is safe. If possible, start by using vegetable matter that you know is not poisonous, such as onion skins.

For the projects in this book, most of the hand-dyeing has been restricted to the materials used to create the sets, rather than the yarn used for the sculptures themselves. But I encourage everyone to develop their knowledge of dyeing, as it is a very useful skill for the needle felter.

THREE BASIC METHODS FOR DYEING WOOL WITH PLANT MATERIALS

• Direct dyeing, in which the dye source and wool fibre are heated together in a water bath. This works well when the dye source is substantive (resists fading) and doesn't require a mordant. Substantive dye sources include pomegranate skin, tea and turmeric.
• Prepare the fibres in advance with a mordant, then dye them in a heated water bath using the plants.
• Place the mordant and dye source together in one dye bath with the wool.

Needles

To streamline the production of felt in the nineteenth century, an English company patented a needle with angled notches along the shaft and engineered a machine with a multiple-needle bed. Individual fibres of carded wool caught in the needle notches and travelled with the downward punch of the needle; when the needle reversed, the fibres were released. Repeated punches increased the matting of the fibres until eventually solid sheets of felt were formed.

HOW TO HOLD THE NEEDLE

Many people are put off needle felting by pricking their fingers, but this is easily solved by changing the way the needle is held.

Keep a finger just above the highest notch (see opposite bottom left). All the notches need to be able to go into the work, so use your finger like a buffer: prod deep enough so that your finger touches the surface of the felt, retreat and repeat. Your brain is aware of this finger's position, so by concentrating on keeping this finger away from your other hand, you will manage not to jab yourself. If you use a holder, keeping all your fingers well away from the pointed end, your brain has a task computing the needle point's position in relation to your other hand, increasing the chances of injury. As you prod, avoid creating an arc by pivoting from the wrist or elbow. If you prod on a curve, you are more likely to break the needle.

CHOOSING YOUR NEEDLE SIZES

The number refers to the wire gauge; the name refers to the arrangement of notches.
Size 32 For creating large components or pieces with coarse wool.
Size 36 For medium wool, coarse wool and pre-felt, to quickly create volume and shape.
Size 38 For applying the surface finish on small objects, using medium to fine wool, and for finer shaping. The puncture marks may show slightly with some fibres.
Sizes 40, 43 and 46 For detailed work and fine finishing without puncture marks.
Crown Has two notches only on the tip.
Star Has a star-shaped cross section with two notches and four edges.

Triangular/Regular Has a triangular cross section with three notches and three edges.
Reverse Has angled notches to draw fibres out on an upwards motion.
Twisted The shaft is twisted for less resist. Use in multiple-needle tools.

OTHER TOOLS

Wooden holder for three needles I keep two ready loaded with size 36 and size 38 needles (see tin, opposite top). Use these to construct larger shapes and achieve strength. Not for small project pieces.
Spring-loaded tool with five needles (centre of tin, opposite) Useful for 2-D work and fine finishing. The lack of prod angle and depth makes it inefficient for 3-D work or shaping large projects. It works well with an inverted brush felting block (see pages 18–19).

NEEDLE STORAGE AND MAINTENANCE

I use a tin (see opposite top left) to store my needles safely. The hinged lid is lined with a sheet of felt to take a range of needles. Other tools are stored in the base, including a telescopic plastic box of needles. A compact version, which is ideal for travelling, is an adapted vintage cigarette case (see opposite top right). It opens to reveal different-sized needles held in felt in both the lid and base.

Other safe storage methods include turned wooden tools, where the needles can be reversed for carrying, or simply pushing the whole needle into your felting block.

If you bend a needle accidentally, you can straighten it by heating it over an open flame and then bending it into shape again.

OPPOSITE BOTTOM, LEFT TO RIGHT
Holding the needle with a finger close to the point reduces the chances of it pricking your fingers; a close-up of a triangular needle with visible notches; a selection of needle sizes, including star and crown needles.

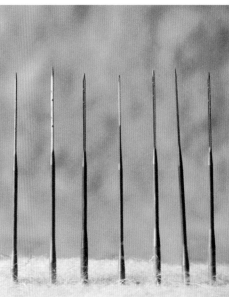

Choosing a felting block

Always work against a felting block, so that when the point of your needle pushes through your work, it is absorbed into the felting block, not your knee or the tabletop. This also prevents needles from being broken against a hard surface. The felting block you choose should be deep enough to absorb the length of whatever needle you are using, allowing you to work on very small or thin pieces of felt.

SPONGE FELTING BLOCK

You may have been encouraged to buy a sponge block, or perhaps one came with a kit you purchased, such as the black rectangular **block 2** shown opposite, but I urge you to try one of the alternatives.

While sponge is an economical way to get started, I find the 'bounce' unpleasant, as it makes my hands ache, and this may put some people off the craft without them ever discovering how much more pleasing the process is when using a felt felting block. However, a sponge will do the job. Upholstery foam is better than a household sponge but both work. All sponges degenerate with continued needling and need to be regularly replaced. When this happens, consider the other options.

INVERTED BRUSH FELTING BLOCK

This option, **block 6**, is light, easy to carry, inexpensive and long-lasting. Wool fibres do not get knotted in between the hairs of the brush. The hairs themselves could be deeper so that all the notches on a size 36 needle could be used. It is a good partner to the spring-loaded multiple-needle tool (see pages 16–17), which tends to have a shortened prod length.

FELT FELTING BLOCK

Personally, I have always preferred to needle felt against felt blocks. Inspired by milliners' wooden blocks and ceramicists' plaster hump moulds, I create blocks of many shapes and sizes, regularly using rectangular, cylindrical and domed blocks.

You can easily make your own selection of blocks using either heavily felted sheeting or pieces of clothing that have been accidentally felted.

Roll a long rectangular strip of felt up into a neat block and prod to secure its shape. This construction is clearly visible in **block 4**, which is a great standard block for small pieces of work.

I have made felting blocks in many sizes and shapes. **Blocks 1** and **3** are both cylindrical and great for making curved surfaces, such as bangles and flower petals. **Block 9** is also a felt cylinder with a great corner for working attachments. **Block 5** is a wedge shape, which I use for neatening fibre-covered wire legs. **Block 10** has a large surface area, which is necessary to make large flat shapes. **Blocks 7** and **8** are filled pebble-shaped blocks, which are very pleasing to use and easier for aching joints.

Develop the habit of repeatedly lifting your work off the block to diminish the risk of entanglement. When your felt block starts to get too firm or shows a dip in the middle, it is simple to offer up some wool fibres or pre-felt circles to fill the dint and prod until they are firmly secured. In this way, I have maintained blocks that have seen many years of service.

As needle felting continues to grow in popularity, felting blocks will be easier to source and will be manufactured in new ways. I have recently developed a filled block with much less resistance, in order to make needle felting easier for those of us with painful joints.

OPPOSITE A range of felting blocks made from sponge, felt and hair.

Getting started

There is something magical about needle felting. I frequently witness expressions of befuddlement on people's faces when they are handed fluffy wool fibres and a needle. This is quickly replaced with delight as the process is revealed. You really can turn piles of fluff into gorgeous sculptures.

The angled notches along the shaft of the needle grab the wool fibres and take them in the direction of each prod. The notches are angled so the wool fibre is left 'in prodded position' and does not make the return journey. Continued prodding makes the entanglement of fibres tighter and tighter, resulting in felt.

This technique has been developed so we can make small items directly from wool fibres or, more frequently, create a basic shape as a starting point for a sculpture. Most of the projects in this book are made by attaching cylinders and balls together and then refining the shape and adding detail until it resembles an animal or bird. I have shown you the methods I use and I encourage you to borrow techniques from other crafts to develop your own work.

STARTING WITH WOOL SHEETING

My preferred method for starting a project is borrowed from paper bead-making. Long rectangles of sheet material are rolled to become cylinders, and long tapered triangles to become spheres. Ovoids start off as a rectangle with a triangular end.

The original sheet of wool may be wet felted, or purchased as wool batting or pre-felt. Pre-felt (perhaps more accurately referred to as proto-felt) is a sheet material that has been very lightly needled and is just starting to resemble felt. The individual fibres are gently entangled, yet it can still be teased apart. Perhaps you have old woollen blankets or accidentally felted sweaters. These can be cut up and used in the same way as pre-felt.

Most of the projects in this book show the basic component parts made by rolling sheet material. While I tend to work in this way, you may prefer an alternative method. Other ways of making the core include:
• Leftover yarn wound into a ball (see opposite bottom right).
• A wet-felted ball (see page 26).
• A polystyrene ball (this will need to be completely covered in wool fibre before you can proceed to any 'shrinking').
• Boiled merino roving, wound or knotted into a ball shape.
• Needle-felted medium or coarse wool.
• Leftover felt offcuts wrapped in wool batting and then needle felted.

BOILING WOOL FIBRES

Consider how carefully you have to launder delicate woollens to prevent them from felting. This is because the high volume of scales on the wool fibres makes them prone to catching on neighbouring fibres. For an impatient felter, this knowledge is useful as it allows you to create partially felted roving that can be used to form the core and surface of your project.

Place some fine roving in a pressure cooker and cover with water. Add a small amount of soap. Soap helps the fibres slide over each other and also provides an alkaline solution, which increases the fibres' ability to swell full of water and uncurl further, encouraging felting. Bring up to full pressure and turn off. Allow to cool before rinsing. An alternative is to use a slow-cook pot, stirring occasionally.

Medium-grade fibres have fewer scales, but it is possible the 'crimp' of the wool offers great 'feltibility' and it is worth treating in this way to see how it responds. You will soon find wools that work well for you.

HOW TO MAKE A BASIC SHAPE

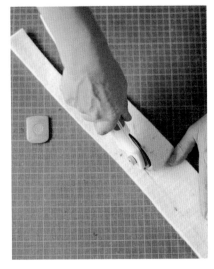

STEP 1 Using tailor's chalk, mark out a long isosceles triangle onto your felt sheeting. This one was 60cm (24in) long and 5cm (2in) across, tapering down to a blunt end 1cm (½in) across.

STEP 2 Roll up the triangle of felt from the fat end to the thin end, making sure the resulting fatness is even on both sides.

STEP 3 Repeatedly needle-prod the 1cm (½in) end to attach it to the ball until secure. You can use a three-needle tool for speed, as I have here.

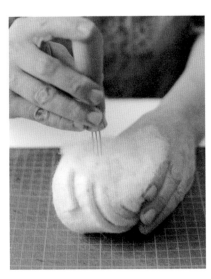

STEP 4 Add some medium fibre and prod to refine the surface.

STEP 5 Continue all over until the ball is even. The same process can be used with a long rectangle to make a cylinder.

VARIATION An alternative method is to wind leftover wool yarn into a ball and apply medium or coarse wool as above.

Sculpting

Once you have created a basic shape, you can start sculpting. You will soon learn to attach wool fibres to a felted object simply by prodding. You can create dips, curves, undercuts, different textures and shapes, just as you would with clay. You can attach two felted pieces together by sandwiching a few fibres in between and prodding them into both bits of felt. The more you prod, the more it felts, shrinking and drawing the two pieces more tightly together – wonderful. There are two basic techniques: prod to shrink and prod to grow.

HOW TO SHRINK

All you need to do is prod. Hold your item on the felting block and prod vertically into the wool ball. The volume will shrink in the direction of the prod, forming a dint in the ball. If you continue working on this dint but angle the needle, you can make a straight-edged hole or even an undercut. A hole is quickly achieved with a size 36 needle and refined with a size 38 needle.

Grooves are very easily achieved with a three-needle tool, and when you have larger amounts to shrink, you can simply cut the wool fibre away with scissors or a craft knife. Felt is very forgiving. If you want to change the position of an attachment, you can cut it off, offer it back in its new position and reattach it. The cut surface can be neatened by adding a new layer of wool fibre and prodding it to attach.

You can flatten an area of the ball simply by prodding. Do this relatively evenly to start with and then with greater concentration in the middle. It is worth practising this with different-sized needles.

HOW TO GROW

You can develop your basic shape by adding wool fibre. You need to add fibre more quickly than your prodding shrinks the work. In order to achieve this, your central core should already be quite firm and the fibre you are adding should be medium-grade wool. I add thin layers of fibre and work to a rhythm: add a wisp; prod, prod, prod, prod; add a wisp; prod, prod, prod; add a wisp, and so on. The wisp only needs to be loosely attached before another wisp is placed on top, as you can prod through a few layers at the same time. This technique helps you control the surface shape more easily.

Alternatively, you can offer up discs and strips of pre-felt to the main work and prod them to attach. Build up layers of pre-felt one on top of another, then refine the surface by adding a layer of wool fibre.

HOW TO JOIN TWO PIECES TOGETHER

Component parts can easily be attached together. If both parts are still quite soft, this means loose strands of wool fibre are available to be prodded into the adjacent shape; push the pieces together and prod through one into the other, and vice versa. Keep moving the work around on your felting block so that you prod from different angles. Try to keep your needle in a vertical position by moving the work, rather than the needle. Sometimes putting the work over the edge of the block helps you access the area you want to shape.

If the two pieces are already quite firm, you need to attach small wisps of wool onto each one, as if you are adding glue to a wooden model or slip to pieces of clay. Then push the two pieces together and prod through to attach. Keep moving the work so that you prod from many directions. The wisps will felt into the work and join the two pieces more and more firmly together. Add more wool to neaten the join.

HOW TO SHRINK

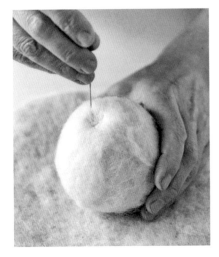

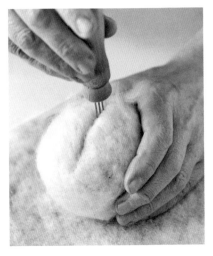

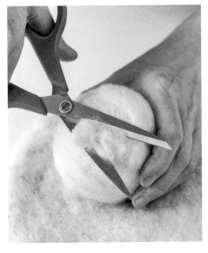

STEP 1 Place your work on a felting block and prod with a size 36 needle. Keep the needle moving vertically, avoiding arcing movements. You will quickly see a dint form. Practise this technique with different needles.

STEP 2 You can quickly create a channel using the three-needle tool. Practise this with different needle sizes.

STEP 3 Needle felting is the most forgiving of crafts. Some alterations are quickly achieved with scissors or a craft knife.

HOW TO GROW

STEP 1 Offer up small wisps of medium-grade wool and prod to attach with a size 36 needle. Add more wool fibres and repeat the process.

STEP 2 Add a small disc of pre-felt to your shape and prod to attach using a size 36 needle.

STEP 3 A few prods will loosely attach a disc, enabling you to offer up a second disc. Prod to secure.

How to structure

Each new needle-felting project needs to have a considered structure. There are many options, some more versatile than others. We need to understand the materials in terms of availability, strength, cost and ethics, and the process in terms of time, enjoyment and skill level.

The importance of individual issues will vary from person to person. Time limitations might dictate, or you may restrict your choices because of environmental concerns. My preferred process is to make individual components out of pre-felt sheeting (local, organic and upcycled) and then join these together to create a figure. Whatever sways your decision, you will need to have a good understanding of how to build strength into your sculptures.

The image below shows a structure made from a needle-felted centre core of coarse wool (Herdwick), with a thin layer of a medium-grade white wool to smooth out the surface before the final layer of fine wool in a red colour. This method is strong, fast and cheap.

Be aware that a spring-loaded multiple-needle tool has less 'reach' than a wooden three-needle tool. If you have a lightly felted ball with a radius greater than the 'reach' of your needle(s), prodding will create a hard 'crust' and a soft centre. This might be fine until you attempt to insert wirework legs. To avoid this, start with a small ball and build it up as necessary; the smaller radius will allow the needle to reach the very centre.

The core should be medium or coarse wool fibre unless the project is very small. I refer to this wool fibre as core wool because of its purpose, but a retailer may not understand such a request so ask for coarse or medium wool fibre.

MAKING SMALL SHAPES SAFELY

But what about making tiny pieces where the needle must travel right through the work? This is where the felting block comes in. You lay your work on the felting block and prod to such a depth that you are making the most of all of the notches on your needle, but the wool fibre is travelling into the felting block. Lifting the work off the block regularly prevents it from becoming attached.

Once you have mastered a few techniques of turning and folding, you will be able to make all kinds of small attachments. Study the images opposite and imagine the possibilities by using different folds. Folding in thirds lengthways makes a long, thin rectangle, which could become a cockscomb, while rolling the rectangle makes small cheeks.

LEFT This shape, like a matryoshka doll, visually explains the change from coarse to medium and then fine wool as a project develops.

THE 'PANCAKE' METHOD

This method is 'best practice' when teaching young students, as it provides a handle, or 'stem', to hold while working on a small item, keeping the fingers safe from prods.

STEP 1 Place a thin layer of fine wool fibre onto the felting block. Prod all over with a size 36 needle.

STEP 2 Lift and turn the wool over. Prod some more, starting to concentrate in the middle and ignoring the perimeter area. Keep lifting, turning and prodding.

STEP 3 Fold the 'pancake' in half and prod to attach it to itself.

STEP 4 Lift and fold a third of the shape in to the middle, and prod again to attach.

STEP 5 Lift and fold again. Prod, leaving the edge fluffy. This fluffy edge is used as a handle when you prod the middle.

STEP 6 The fluff also helps you attach the small object to the main sculpture. It can be tidied up after attachment.

Wet felting

A well-trodden path to needle felting is via wet felting and, indeed, they make good bedfellows. Needle felting offers the wet felter greater control over the end result and a more direct route to creating three-dimensional objects. Uneven areas and errors from wet felting are easily rectified by needle felting.

WET FELTING BY HAND

The basic premise of wet felting is to agitate wet wool fibres in an alkaline solution. Each wool fibre is able to absorb three times its weight in water and, when full, the surface scales tilt out to the maximum degree possible, catching the scales on adjacent fibres. Continuous rubbing encourages the fibres to knit together and become felt. I regularly use this method to create pieces of wet-felt sheeting and wet-felt balls, which I then refine by needle felting.

To wet felt a ball, take a quantity of wool fibre and misalign the strands. Fold and roll the wool into a wad and hold it between the palms of your hands.

Working over a bowl of hot, soapy water, dunk the wad of fibre into the water. Cover your palms in soap suds and start to gently roll the wad between your palms. Do not apply any significant pressure, just gently roll it around and around, keeping it hot, wet and soapy. Keep rolling. You should feel it starting to felt within a couple of minutes. Continue doing this until the felt is relatively firm.

Wash the soap away with clean, cold water. Then repeat the process, returning the ball to the hot, soapy water and continuing to roll it between your soapy palms. You will feel the ball shrinking and stiffening. Rinse thoroughly.

At this wet stage, you can roll the ball into an ovoid or a sausage shape and the shape will be retained when it dries. This is a great way to make eggs and limbs.

THE OBERON POD

I was taught to make vessels by wet felting over a plastic sheet 'resist' and then reshaping the work to become three-dimensional. I find this process too time-consuming and have developed the pine-cone method (see opposite) as a quick alternative. Using a pine cone's natural process of opening and closing pleases me. I refer to the vessel made by this method as an 'Oberon Pod'.

I am sharing this technique with you as it's a lovely introduction to felting and particularly useful for children's workshops. The resulting vessel can be made into all kinds of projects, such as nests for swallow chicks (see pages 64–5). I hope you will find it to be a useful addition to your felting repertoire.

USING YOUR WASHING MACHINE

To wet felt using your washing machine, first misalign the wool fibres, folding and rolling them into a wad. Soak the wad in soapy water before placing and sealing it tightly inside a plastic bag. Prick a few holes in the plastic and place it in the washing/drying machine. Try a hot wash and a warm dry cycle.

Alternative methods include knotting the soaked fibres into a pair of tights (pantyhose) or sealing them in a two-part plastic mould drilled with holes. Then wash and dry as above.

The variables here are the breed of sheep, grade of wool, alkalinity of the water and length and temperature of the wash.

THE OBERON POD: PINE-CONE METHOD

STEP 1 Take an open pine cone and gently wrap it in fine wool fibre until it is completely covered. You will need about 5g (¼oz) of fine wool fibre for each pine cone.

STEP 2 Dunk the wrapped pine cone into hot, soapy water and, with soapy hands, start to gently roll it between your palms. Continue to roll, occasionally dunking it into hot, soapy water and then cold, clean water. You will feel the wool begin to felt. Continue until firmly felted, then rinse in cold, clean water.

STEP 3 Leave the felt to dry and the pine cone to close. When it is completely dry, use scissors to cut the top of the felt off. Trim away the felt around the top of the pine cone and carefully remove it.

STEP 4 Neaten the pod by needle felting. You can alter the size and shape at this stage. The finished pods were put into a pressure cooker (no longer used for food) with pine cones and onion skins, brought up to full pressure, turned off and allowed to cool. The rich brown colour is the result.

Adding colour

Once you have built and shaped your creature, you need to add surface colour and pattern. If you have coloured merino, your wool fibres may be very neatly arranged in a parallel formation. Some people wrap this straight around a body and prod it into place to secure it. These lines remain visible and the effect on the finished item should be considered. Think about drawing an apple; which way would you have the direction of the shading? This has an impact on the success of the final drawing, and the direction of the wool fibres is the equivalent in needle felting.

ADDING NATURAL SURFACE COLOUR

To avoid creating obvious lines on your finished piece, take small amounts of merino and agitate them between your fingers to misalign all the fibres until they appear completely random. Alternatively, you can use a carding comb for this task.

Offer tiny wisps of the colour up to the body and prod to attach. Use a size 38 needle to do this, even though you might leave visible holes on the surface. Then change to a size 40 needle to finish and reduce the effect of the holes.

If you are covering a large area, as with the gull project (see page 132), you may like to use a multiple-needle tool to speed up this process. Remember, the plastic tools are restricted in the angles you can prod but useful for rapid solid-colour coverage.

I also add thin wisps of wool, layer upon layer, in different tones, in a way that is reminiscent of adding layers of watercolour or translucent glaze in decorative painting. This helps to give a consistency to the finish and a more subtle grading of colour.

INTERNAL COLOURS

Needle felting offers the opportunity to reveal a new surface by cutting into a piece of work. Cutting a cross section through a heavily felted object exposes a lovely dotted surface. I often use this on the snouts of hedgehogs and mice. You build up the snout to be larger than you need, layering colour upon colour. When you cut the felt away to create the snout shape, you will find the surface is made up of beautiful minuscule dots.

DYEING AND BLENDING

Dyeing batches of fibres in the same dye bath but soaking them for varying lengths of time achieves graded tones of the same colour. This is great for fur and skin tones.

LEFT The subtle colouring of the hedgehog's snout can be achieved following step 3 on page 104, or by cutting into the solid felt, as mentioned in Internal Colours here.

HOW TO ADD COLOUR

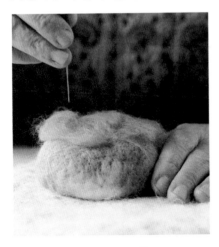

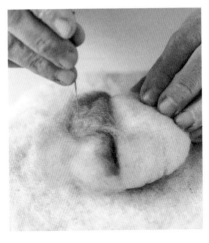

ALL-OVER COLOUR Offer up some misaligned wisps of fine wool fibre in the colour of your choice and prod to attach them to your sculpture. Note the holes left by your needle and adjust the needle size accordingly.

CREATING SUBTLE GRADING OF COLOURS I build up very fine layers of very fine wool batting, where the fibres are misaligned, using a very fine needle – size 38 or 40. I may add five or six tones of a single colour to create a fine finish.

CREATING A NEAT COLOUR CHANGE Offer up a thin layer of fine wool and prod to attach along an imagined line. Lift the unattached fibre from one side and fold it back over the line. Smooth it down and prod to secure.

CREATING DOTS Offer up a little coloured wool fibre to the work. Push the needle in, and lift it up and down without removing the point from the work. When the fibre is attached, but with fibre still remaining outside the work, remove the needle and trim the excess fibre flat with the surface.

CREATING A LINE Create a series of dots close together, as described on the left. When the fibres are trimmed back, you will reveal a very neat line. Try making dots with different grades of wool and sizes of needles. You can create delicate to medium-sized dots very quickly using this technique.

Creating texture

Many of my workshop participants arrive already knowledgeable in another craft area, most frequently needlecraft, knitting, millinery or ceramics. Their prior experience is often evident in their approach to surface texture. Appliqué, sprigging, fabric manipulation and stamping are all techniques we borrow from different disciplines and bring into our felt work.

The nature of the surface itself is highly dependent on the materials being used. Some wools are incredibly lustrous, others extremely curly or resiliently straight. Drawing on our knowledge of fibres and techniques and taking inspiration from the world around us, we can achieve endless different textures. For example, a close-up of a snail or starfish reveals an amazingly textured surface. I have tried to imply something of this by using a twizzle-bump method (see pages 130–1). Another designer might approach the same task with an appliqué technique, cutting small amounts of pre-felt and offering them up repeatedly to the body. An embroidery enthusiast, on the other hand, may work a series of French knots all over the surface.

It wasn't appropriate to assume that readers would bring knowledge of other crafts to the projects in this book, so I have kept the designs free from embroidery, knitting and dyeing techniques. I hint at such cross-pollination of skills in the set designs, with rag-rug skies, knitted clifftops and stitched furrows, and encourage you to bring your craft knowledge to bear. I would love to see decorative stitching on the owl, a knitted surface on the sheep or beading on the starfish. Let your imagination soar. Blend new and old methods, gradually building up your repertoire.

Here are a few suggestions (see opposite):

1 Spun 3-ply yarn is prodded to attach it to a piece of felt. The yarn is then 'unspun' between your fingers and the new, thinner strands retain some of the kinks.

2 This natural soya bean yarn is very fine and lustrous. It takes up dye well but in a different way from wool.

3 This bumpy surface is created by offering up wisps of fine wool fibre to the surface. Wherever you want to make a bump, cover the surface with a wisp of fine fibre, dot the circumference of the desired bump and then push the overlapping fibre inside the circumference and prod. The bumps can be gently raised or made of a different sheen or colour from the background (see Creating dots, page 29).

4 Natural silk has incredible sheen and is available in a good range of colours.

5 This is similar to the process of fabric manipulation, where a repeated action results in an effect that implies a completely new fabric. A piece of roving is attached at the top of an imagined vertical line, then a row of circles is prodded into it, leaving the middle of each bump unattached. The next row is worked to 'interconnect' the circles.

6 This is Blue Leicester fleece, which has a natural curl.

7 The striped effect is created with strips of silk against raw fleece.

8 This is stocking-stitch knitting prodded to attach it onto a felt backing.

9 Wool yarn has been cut into strips and prodded to attach it, to resemble stitches.

Creating character

I am tempted to record people's 'ooohs' and 'aaahs' when they see my felted animals at craft fairs. I like to give each creature its own individual character and am richly rewarded by people's joyful response.

We tend to impose human emotions onto animals and, while this book isn't meant to anthropomorphize the creatures, I knowingly employ techniques to increase the 'aaah' factor. These include using disproportionately large heads and eyes; wide, forward-facing eyes; full cheeks and lips; and limbs in carefully considered proportions. All are aimed at fooling us into thinking the animal is young. After all, we are hot-wired to look after our own babies, and this is an instinct we extend to other species' young. I make a sketch to check that my assumptions work. Should the eyes be very high up and far apart like a nanny goat? Or low down the nose and close together like a little bichon frise pup? It's not that one is wrong or right; it's about being in control of the character you create, rather than leaving it to chance.

MAKING EYES

Eyes are crucial. You may choose to buy top-of-the-range taxidermy eyes, or even make eyes with resin. For the projects in this book, however, I have kept to methods that a beginner can easily achieve, including needle felting, air-drying clay, papier-mâché (paper pulp) and beads. I encourage you to develop these skills, as they will enable you to create your own style.

Needle felting an eye The simplest of eyes is a needle-felted dot (see Creating dots, page 29). Next, we have five dots in a row, to create a curved, 'smiling' eye or an 'asleep' eye. The sheepdog, polar bear and fox (see pages 66, 80 and 98) all have needle-felted eyes. They are quick and simple, and can be substituted into the other projects if you need a faster option.

Beady eyes A little black glass or hematite bead is simple and effective. They look 'right'. To attach the bead securely, prod a socket almost as deep as the bead and, using a doll needle and strong thread, stitch the bead in place. Stitch repeatedly from one eye to the other and through the back of the head or under the chin, working in a triangle formation to ensure the beads are secured.

Moulded eyes You can mould eyes out of traditional clay, air-drying clay or paper. A fired-clay bead can be formed around a nichrome wire loop. This enables it to be hung from a bead frame for glaze firing and later doubles as a stitching anchor when securing it within the eye socket. Air-drying clay and papier-mâché (paper pulp) can be moulded around a foil core to speed up the drying process. Many brands of air-drying clay can be sanded smooth before being painted, or you can use felt-tip pens to add colour and detail.

Rolled paper beads Roll long, thin, tapered triangles of paper around a hollow cotton-bud (Q-tip) stick and refine the surface with fine papier-mâché (paper-pulp) layers. The snipped cotton-bud (Q-tip) stick forms the core of the bead.

Felt eyelids Larger eyes can be held in position with felt eyelids. Make an eye socket large enough to take two-thirds of the eye and push it in. Make two small, flat sausages of felt on your felting block and offer them up to the work as eyelids, prodding them repeatedly on either side of the eye to attach them and hold the eyeballs securely in place.

OPPOSITE While it is possible to purchase many forms of model eyes, it is very rewarding to make your own from paper, clay or wood.

Wirework

Used to make components such as legs, antlers and tails, wirework is a great skill to enhance your needle-felting projects. Wire can be bought from florists, garden stores, electricians and the bead-making section of craft retailers. Its strength and malleability need to be weighed up against its appearance.

APPEARANCE
Coloured wire is available from beading retailers in a range of thicknesses (gauge) and strengths. Electrical suppliers offer plastic-coated and cotton-coated wire, which are much easier to bend with your fingers. I like to home-dye cotton-covered wire for birds' legs. A small pair of pliers will enable you to work with thicker, firmer wire.

STRENGTH
Choose a wire and type of structure strong enough to hold the weight of the project. Sometimes we twist more than one strand together, to increase the strength of the wire, and add internal structures to projects to increase their stability.

TAILS
The tails of some animals benefit from being wired (see the sheepdog and fox, pages 66 and 98). Create a wire loop to embed into the animal's body. A secure joint is created by prodding through this loop with your needle. The cut ends need to be twisted back around the wire and safely covered with felt.

SMALL BIRDS
A tiny chick (see page 54) will have very little weight so it will be adequate to create legs with a simple, U-shaped bend that allows them to be a belly's width apart, which can be secured within the underside of the body. Ensure the felt body is tightly gripping the internal wire by extensive prodding.

MEDIUM-SIZED BIRDS
A larger bird will not be stable with the U-shaped bend method, as the weight of the body will cause it to pitch forwards or backwards as it pivots around the wire embedded in the belly. To counteract this, attach a circle of wire on the horizontal plane to the top of the legs and insert the whole thing into the belly (see the owl, page 124). Prod the felt tightly around the circle to make a strong attachment.

MOUNTING BIRDS
Wire legs also need to be securely attached to a mounting block, such as a woodturner's block. Tap a nail through each wire foot to attach it to the block. An additional wire loop might help (see the oystercatcher, page 141).

ANTLERS
As antlers only have to support their own weight, they can be made out of thinner wire. However, the wire that spans the antlers still needs to be embedded deeply into the head of the animal in order to achieve some strength.

GETTING STARTED
If working with wire is completely new to you, I suggest you snip off 30cm (12in) or so of malleable wire, fold it in half and see how you can twist the two strands into each other. With a little practice, you will be able to make the twist very regular and do this very quickly.

Once this simple technique is mastered, you can start to consider tackling some more complex shapes (see overleaf). You will soon be making tiny mouse feet with three wee toes, cloven-hoofed herding animals and multi-branched antlers without a second thought.

OPPOSITE This reindeer (see page 84) has the complex, multi-point antlers of a mature stag. If you are new to wirework, start by making simple three-point antlers (see page 37), as would be seen on a young reindeer.

MAMMAL'S LEGS – ONE PAIR

This structure enables you to adjust the length of the legs to ensure the animal stands up, before embedding the wire securely and seamlessly inside your felt model. Each leg is a double strand of wire, which builds in more strength. Once you have mastered the simple wrapping technique, you can make more complicated shapes, such as a two-toed sheep or a three-toed mouse.

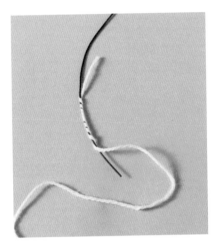

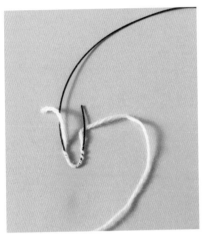

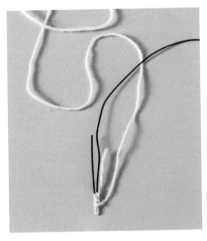

STEP 1 For legs a thumb's length long, wind yarn around a 30cm (12in) piece of wire, starting one thumb's length in from the end.

STEP 2 Fold the wire back on itself one thumb's length in from the end. The yarn should cover the wire completely, right on the fold.

STEP 3 Wind the yarn around the now double-thickness wire as neatly as you can, working down to the bend and back up again.

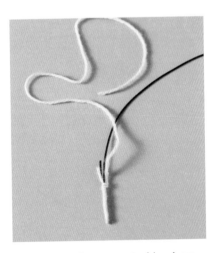

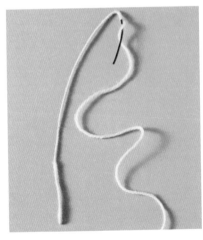

STEP 4 Continue to wind back up the wire. With practice, you can create a pleasing rhythm to the winds. Work right up to a thumb's length from the other end.

STEP 5 A thumb's length from the end, repeat step 2 above to fold the wire back on itself and form a second leg. Make sure you have wound the yarn just past the bend before squeezing the

wires together. As in step 3 above, wind the yarn around the double thickness of wire, working back towards the middle.

Secure the end of the yarn by prodding it into the wrapped fibres with your size 38 felting needle, being careful to avoid the wire so you don't break the needle.

You now have two double-thickness legs (for either the front or rear of the animal), joined by a length of single wire. This central wire is used to create an 'adjustable bend', which enables you to alter the length of each leg easily.

NOTE For examples of adjustable bends formed from yarn-covered wire, see the sheepdog, sheep, goat and fox on pages 66, 70, 94 and 98.

BIRD'S FEET

It is helpful to consider the foot design separately from the support structure within the body, but the legs are made in a pair from one piece of wire and you need enough wire between them to span the underbelly. This basic design ensures the cut ends are embedded inside the body and it is easy to adapt – perhaps by adding a knot for a knee or a loop to attach to a mounting block.

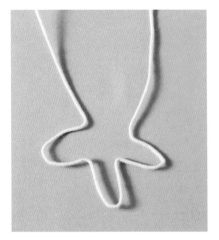

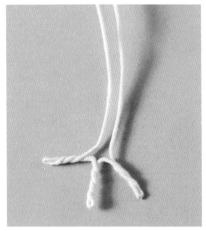

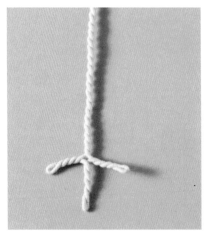

STEP 1 Bend the wire into this pattern to start a three-toed bird's foot. A simple adaptation is possible to create four toes.

STEP 2 Twist the wires together to form each toe. You can either leave the wire raw or wind wool fibre around it.

STEP 3 Continue to twist all the way up the leg. Leave space to span the underbelly and then repeat the process to make the second leg.

ANTLERS

The structure of the antlers is a variation on the bird's leg. Whereas the bird's toes all meet at the ankle, here, there is a series of single extensions from a main horn. A young deer has simple three-point horns; each year its horns become larger with more extensions.

STEP 1 As the antlers use a surprisingly long piece of wire, it is a good idea to bend the whole shape before you begin winding with wool or twisting.

STEP 2 I start twisting from the tips of the horns, working back to the middle.

STEP 3 Some designs are based on winding wool fibre around the wire. A different look is achieved if the wire is twisted before it is covered.

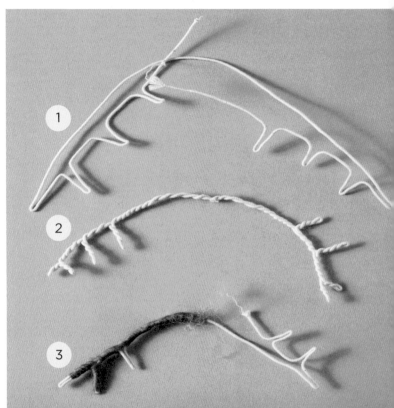

Creating sets

I have loved creating the naturalistic little sets for the characters in this book, using a combination of crafts as well as bought and found objects. I think of it as part of the storytelling process and an extension of a childhood hobby.

PAPIER-MÂCHÉ STRUCTURES
I used three methods to create the structures before deciding on the surface covering:
• Rip, cut and roll corrugated cardboard pieces into shapes and tape them together with masking tape.
• Pinch small or thin curved shapes from kitchen foil.
• Roll, twist and scrunch structures out of sheets of newspaper.

PAPIER-MÂCHÉ SURFACE TEXTURES
Surface with one of the following methods:
• A mash of bathroom tissue mixed with glue (70% PVA : 30% wallpaper paste).

• Layer upon layer of newspaper strips that have been soaked in glue (30% PVA: 70% wallpaper paste).

There are many suitable glues but my preferred glue is a mix of PVA glue and wallpaper paste. The PVA is incredibly strong, while the wallpaper paste reduces the annoying stickiness.

Layers of newspaper enable you to create a smooth finish, whereas a pulp mash allows you to apply texture to the surface.

Finally, add colour. The obvious choice is paint, but I also use various found objects and fibres, such as birch sloughs, hemp and autumn leaves.

FOUND OBJECTS
Some sets are enhanced by the addition of natural objects - for example, the moss-covered rocks in the sheep project (see page 70) and the autumn seeds and pods used for the hedgehog's set (see page 102). Or you may be inspired by the marbles used to represent ice (see page 8).

CREATING GRASS (LEFT)
Heavy wool felt batting was acid-dyed and cut into segment shapes. The flat edge of each segment was then offered up to a piece of wool felt batting and prod-attached. A second segment was placed partially in front of the first and prod-attached to the batting and the first segment. This was repeated until the batting was covered.

CREATING A CLIFFTOP (OPPOSITE)
I knitted some spare Donegal tweed yarn and dyed it green with acid dye. I then needle-felted green medium-weight wool fibre into it in patches and cut it to shape. The felted edges prevent the knitting from unravelling when it is cut.

SILVER BIRCHES

Twisted sheets of newspaper were covered in smooth papier-mâché (paper pulp). When dried solid, they were painted white. Silver birch sloughs were collected in the spring and glued onto the 'trunks' using thin PVA glue.

MUSHROOMS

The gills of the mushroom were created by making a cardboard disc with a central hole. Wool yarn was wound through the hole and around the cardboard repeatedly until the cardboard was covered and there was enough wool thickness at the outer edge to attach a hemisphere of felt by needle felting. This became the mushroom cap. A cylinder of felt was attached to the central hole to make the stalk.

SHELLS

A very long, thin cylinder of felt was created around a wire core, by wrapping the wire with medium-grade wool fibre and prodding it until it felted. One end was fattened by adding more wool fibre, and the cylinder was then gently tapered towards the thin end. Starting at the thin end, the whole shape was then wound up to create a whorl, which was prodded to secure it in place.

PEBBLES

Small wads of merino fibres in different shades of grey were wet felted, then squashed and allowed to dry in a flattened shape. When dry, their surfaces were refined by needle felting and strands of a different-coloured fibre were attached to each one to form the 'veins'.

TREE (METHOD 1)

Some single pieces of wire were wound with medium-grade brown wool fibres. These were then grouped together around a core of felt and prodded to attach. For the tree on page 39, the wires were extended to create roots, and more wool fibre was added to accentuate the foliage. The trunk was made to be the full height of the tree.

Blended medium-grade wool fibres were needle felted into shapes similar to an orange segment, offered up to the trunk of the tree and prodded to attach.

The shape was then extenuated by adding more fibre, where required.

TREES (METHOD 2)

For the left-hand tree, an individual leaf was created from blended medium-grade green wool fibres. A piece of wire had a loop and twist made at one end. The loop was offered up to the leaf against a felting block, and more fibres were carefully prodded onto the leaf, attaching the wire securely. Wool was wound down the length of the wire and the sharp end bent back and bound in wool. Twelve leaves with wires were grouped together and bound to make a narrow trunk.

The right-hand tree is identical but initially a ball was made and cut to insert the loop of wire.

HORSE-CHESTNUT CASE

To create the prickly horse-chestnut case, a sheet of kitchen foil, about the size of this book, was ripped from a roll and folded into quarters. This was slowly fashioned into a dish shape by bending the edges inwards. The foil was gently manipulated until a basic shape had been formed. This was covered with layers of newspaper papier-mâché (paper pulp), both inside and out, and left to dry thoroughly. Layers of glued newspaper were wrapped around lengths of plastic straw, which were cut at a sharp angle. These were attached with newspaper to the horse-chestnut case. This process was repeated until the surface was covered in plenty of prickles. Once dry, the case was painted green.

DANDELIONS

These lovely dandelion heads were made from pom-poms. Medium-grade green wool was used for one half of the pom-poms (made using a pom-pom tool or a doughnut-shaped piece of cardboard) and various wool fibres for the other half, to represent dandelion petals. The pom-poms were secured with fine wire. The green half was needle felted to become the sepals and stem, and the top half was allowed to 'bloom'. The wire stem was covered with florist's green tape.

FABRIC BACKGROUNDS

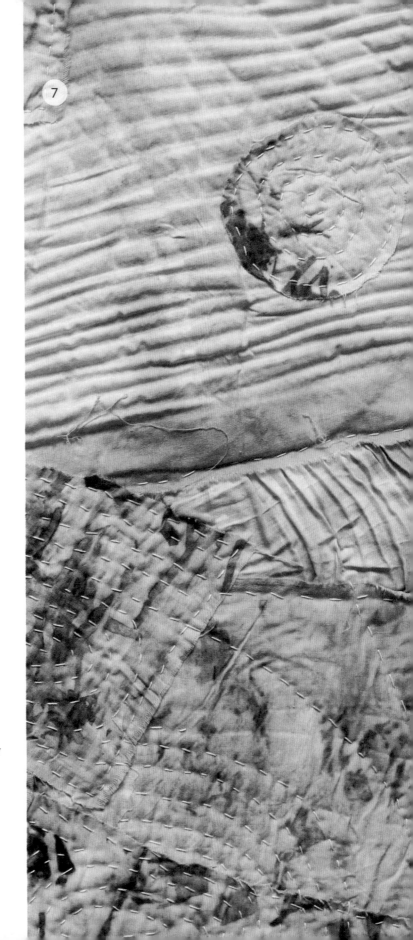

The backdrops and many of the base panels hint at natural phenomena.

1 Red-onion skins were cut into squares and rectangles before being wrapped in a bundle of cotton and tied with string. This was popped in the pressure cooker, brought up to full pressure and allowed to cool overnight.

2 Layers of sheer fabric were Kantha-stitched onto felt batting, to encapsulate random strips of felt.

3 Various white materials were cut or torn into long strips 2cm (½in) wide and prodded onto a hessian (burlap) backing using a rag-rugging technique. The materials used included netting, plastic, sheers and cotton sheeting.

4 Torn green strips were sewn with linen thread to represent the furrows trodden by cows on a hillside, or the winter wheat just making its way through the soil.

5 Cotton sheeting was rust-dyed in the garden for two weeks and then overdyed with Scots pine cones.

6 Hemp fibre was needle felted to attach it onto a hessian (burlap) backing.

7 Pieces of cotton have been dyed with onion skins, using a variety of techniques, before being kantha-stitched onto felt batting to represent autumn fields. Suitable mordants are soya-bean milk or alum, and the fabric can be dyed in a pressure cooker or open pot.

The ridged effect is called *arashi*. To do this, wrap the cotton around a cylinder that will withstand 100°C (212°F). Wind string around the cotton, leaving a gap of 1cm (½in) between each wind. When you get to the top of the cylinder, push the cotton down into itself so the string now has no gaps; the cotton fabric sticks out between the string binds, which act as a resist to the dye, while the rest of the cotton fabric becomes coloured. Stand this in the dye bath, add onion skin and heat. Allow it to simmer for an hour before turning it off and leaving it to cool.

FARMLAND

I have had some very happy years living on farms and the way of life has influenced me greatly. On a farm every new season brings its own routines and pleasures. There is a satisfaction to be taken in work patterns that follow the rhythm of the year, so I maintain this seasonal approach by dyeing fibres in the spring and summer, and felting and stitching in the winter.

SUSSEX HEN & CHICK

When I was a wee lass, I would delight in collecting bantam eggs on Grandpa Charlie's farm and, 30 years later, my son Charlie was lucky enough to collect eggs from his grandfather's hens. It is fabulous to witness a child's joy and care in collecting the eggs for breakfast.

CREATING THE SET

Hand-painted and distressed wooden panels make the coop, with a 'straw' base of hemp and hessian (burlap).

HEN

EQUIPMENT AND MATERIALS

- Felting block
- Needles: sizes 36 and 38; three-needle tool (size 38)
- Scissors; doll needle and strong thread
- Pre-felt: 40 x 40cm (16 x 16in)
- Ball of yarn/non-woven fabric strips: 16cm (6¼in) diameter
- Wool fibre: 100g (4oz) medium in white; 25g (1oz) fine in white, black, tan, yellow, pink and red
- Two black glass beads for the eyes

↑ STEP 1 Cover the ball of yarn or non-woven fabric strips with medium white wool fibre, using a three-needle tool with size 38 needles.

← STEP 2 Refine the ball shape and add more medium wool fibre to the neck and tail areas.

← STEP 3 Make a tail mound and neck area by adding pre-felt and prodding to attach. Add more medium wool fibre, continuing to build these areas upwards and outwards.

↓ STEP 4 For the tail, make a disc out of a double layer of pre-felt, and prod to refine the shape with additional medium wool fibre.

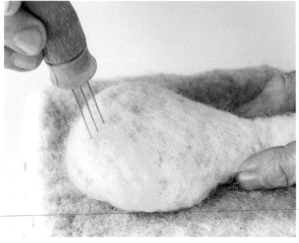

← STEP 5 The tail feathers are cut from a single layer of pre-felt and prodded with additional white fine fibre to refine them into a feather shape. Make 12 tail feathers.

→ STEP 6 Starting with a size 36 needle and then changing to a size 38 needle, give each tail feather a black tip.

← STEP 7 Change to a size 36 needle and prod to attach the tail disc to the tail area of the hen's body, using medium white wool fibre.

↑ STEP 8 Attach each tail feather individually to the tail disc, overlapping them to create a fan arrangement and checking the height of each.

↑ STEP 9 Using pre-felt, make a ball of 4cm (1½in) diameter for the head and a cylinder of 1cm (½in) diameter and 5cm (2in) length for the neck. Prod to attach them together.

→ STEP 10 Change to a size 38 needle. Using the 'pancake' method on pages 25 and tan fine wool fibre, make a thin, flat circle and fold it repeatedly to make a cone shape for the beak. Prod to attach it to the centre of the hen's face.

← STEP 11 Refine the head shape further, flattening the sides and adding the facial details as follows. Prod two eye sockets big enough to accept the beads for the eyes. Add fine yellow wool fibre around the eye sockets. Add pink fibre between the eyes and the beak. Make a red wattle using the 'pancake' method, as before, and attach it by prodding.

↓ STEP 12 Change to a size 36 needle and, using white medium fibre, prod to attach the neck to the body.

← STEP 13 Change to a size 38 needle and use the 'pancake' method to make a crown from red fine wool fibre. Refine the shape with a size 36 needle and then a size 38 needle.

← STEP 14 Prod to attach the crown to the top of the head. Then sew in the eye beads using a doll needle and strong thread.

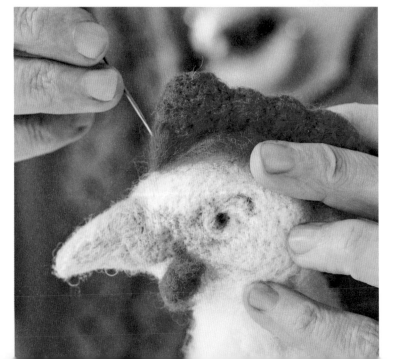

→ STEP 15 Change to a size 36 needle and use pre-felt to make a series of small neck feathers, about 3 x 1.5cm (1¼ x ⅝in). Using a size 38 needle, refine them with white fine fibre and add black tips. Prod to attach them to the hen's neck.

↓ STEP 16 Cut two egg-shaped wings, approximately 7 x 12cm (2¾ x 4¾in), from a double layer of pre-felt. Using a three-needle tool with size 38 needles, prod-attach fine white wool fibre; prod to refine the shape until the wings are really quite firm. Attach the first wing to the body by prodding at the shoulder and along the back. Repeat for the other wing on the other side of the hen.

→ FINISHED HEN You now have your very own Sussex hen.

CHICK

EQUIPMENT AND MATERIALS

- Felting block
- Needles: sizes 36, 38 and 40
- Craft knife
- Doll needle and strong thread
- Wool fibre: 25g (1oz) medium in white; 5g (¼oz) fine in white, tan, yellow and cream
- Wet-felted ovoid (egg shape), 7cm (2¾in) long
- Fine wire for the legs: 50cm (19¾in), twisted into a U-shaped leg structure with three toes on each foot (see page 37)
- Two black glass beads for eyes

↑ STEP 1 Using a size 36 needle, offer wisps of medium wool fibre onto your egg shape and prod to attach. Repeat this process, enlarging the head area and the tail area. Continue to prod, adding medium wool fibre to refine the shape.

↑ STEP 2 Using your craft knife, cut a deep slit into the underside of the belly area and push the U-shaped middle of the wire legs into the cut. Hold the cut shut with your fingers and prod through it to secure it closed. Prod all over to refine the shape.

→ STEP 3 Prod two eye sockets. Stitch a black bead securely into each socket using a doll needle and strong thread. Change to a size 38 needle and, following the 'pancake' method on page 25, make a small tan beak and attach it centrally to the face. Refine the shape.

→ STEP 4 Using a size 38 or 40 needle, attach the fine yellow wool to the back, head and wing areas. Attach the cream wool to the breast and underbelly regions.

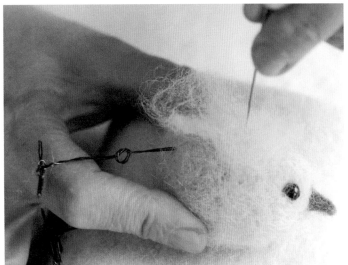

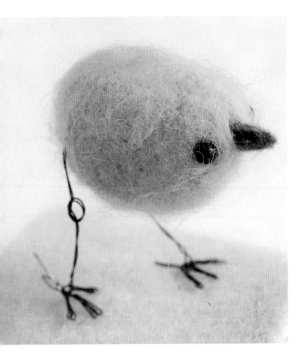

↑ STEP 5 Bend the legs into a supporting position and alter until your chick stands up.

→ FINISHED CHICK Make a clutch of chicks - they are always happier with some company.

AYRSHIRE COW

Grandpa Charlie bred Ayrshire cows (brown and whites), including many rosette winners and even a champion. Years later, they still have a special place in my heart.

CREATING THE SET
The fields are made of felt, with felt trees (see pages 38 and 42), and the background is a partially completed rag-rug.

EQUIPMENT AND MATERIALS
- Felting block
- Needles: sizes 36, 38 and 40
- Craft knife
- Wire snips and pliers
- Pre-felt: 30 x 40cm (12 x 16in)
- Wool fibre: 50g (2oz) medium in white; 25g (1oz) fine in white and reddish brown; 5g (¼oz) fine in pale pink and black
- Medium craft wire for the legs: 1 x 20cm (8in) long and 1 x 26cm (10¼in) long (see page 36)

↑ STEP 1 Create the component parts from pre-felt. The body, head and neck are cylinders of the following diameter-to-length proportions: 4 : 9cm (1½ : 3½in), 1.5 : 4cm (⅝ : 1½in) and 1.5 : 1.5cm (⅝ : ⅝in). Cover the wires with yarn. Use the longer piece to make an adjustable bend with a central loop and bend the shorter piece into a simple curve, as shown.

← STEP 2 Offer up the shorter wire legs to one end of the body cylinder, lay a small strip of pre-felt over the wire and prod it to attach loosely, using a size 36 needle. Consider the legs-to-body proportions and move the wire up or down accordingly. Prod to attach it more securely. Loosely attach the longer legs to the other end of the body. Stand the body up and alter the individual leg lengths as necessary, then prod to attach the legs firmly.

STEP 3 Using the edge of your felting block, wrap medium wool fibre around each leg to give shape to the thigh area, the knee and the hock. Decide which are the front legs and which are the back legs, then bend the wire to create a knee joint in the back legs. Prod carefully, avoiding the wire, to attach the wool to wool. Keep moving the leg into different positions to access different parts of it. Remember, the hooves are quite large. Prod until the wool is tight and secure.

STEP 4 Having given each leg some shape, work on the area where the legs join the body. Pieces of pre-felt may help you here or you could carry on adding more medium wool fibre. Build up the tummy area and add a shapely udder.

STEP 5 Change to a size 38 needle and fine wool fibre. Prod reddish brown and white patches onto your cow.

STEP 6 Colour the udder with pale pink fibre and add four teats.

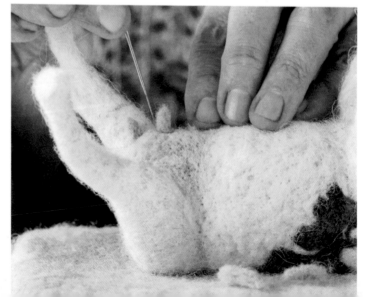

← STEP 7 Change to a size 36 needle. To join the head to the neck, first add a wisp of medium wool fibre to each cylinder, then hold them together and prod from one to the other. Use the edge of the block to enable your prodding hand to stay as vertical as possible. Prod to refine the forehead area and create a lovely long curve leading down to the muzzle. Change to a size 38 needle to add brown patches and a pale pink nose.

↓ STEP 8 Add white eyes with black pupils and give the nose black nostrils.

← STEP 9 To make the tail, roll a small amount of white and reddish brown fine wool between your palms and prod against a felting block to secure, leaving wisps loose at one end. Cut the tail to length and prod to attach it to the rear of the cow. Change to a size 36 needle to attach the head. Add a wisp of medium fibre to the base of the neck, offer it up to the body and prod through both parts to join them securely. Change to a size 38 needle to neaten the joint with a little fine wool fibre.

→ FINISHED COW Refine all over with a size 38 needle and then a size 40 needle, as required, and your lovely Ayrshire cow is complete.

SWALLOW & CHICK

A charming folk tale gives an imaginative explanation for bird migration: swallows dive into the river in the autumn and spend the winter months in an underwater world before re-emerging in the spring.

CREATING THE SET

Papier-mâché (paper pulp) on hessian (burlap) makes the backdrop for the nest pods (see Wet felting on page 26).

SWALLOW

EQUIPMENT AND MATERIALS

- Felting block
- Needles: sizes 36 and 38; three-needle tool (size 38); crown needle size 38
- Craft knife or small scissors
- Doll needle and thread
- Pre-felt: 30 x 40cm (12 x 16in)
- Wool fibre: 100g (4oz) medium in white; 25g (1oz) fine in white, tan, ruby red, royal blue and black
- Two black glass beads for the eyes

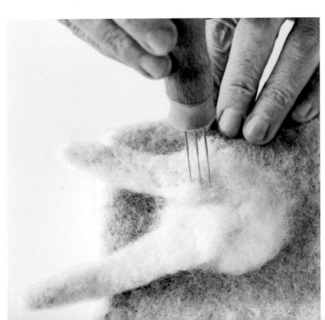

↑ STEP 1 Make the component parts. Beak: make from tan fine wool fibre; head: pre-felt ball 3cm (1¼in) diameter; body: pre-felt ball 6cm (2½in) diameter; two wings: cut double layers of pre-felt measuring 15cm (6in) diagonally across the wing to the tip; tail: disc 5cm (2in) diameter; two tail feathers: cut double layers of pre-felt 6cm (2½in) long.

← STEP 2 Using a three-needle tool with size 38 needles, prod to attach the tail feathers to the tail disc. Add white medium fibre and prod to refine the shape.

STEP 3 Using a size 36 needle, prod to attach the body to the non-feathered end of the tail disc. Add white medium fibre and prod to refine the shape.

STEP 4 Prod to attach the neck to the head; you can then hold the head securely and work on its shape safely. Changing to a size 38 needle, colour the cheeks and chin in ruby red. Attach the beak to the centre front of the head.

STEP 5 Change to a size 36 needle to attach the head to the body, adding white medium wool fibre to make the joint secure and neat.

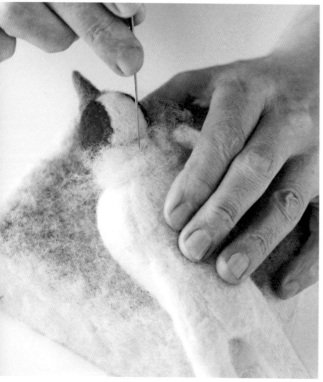

STEP 6 Offer up a wing to one side of the body and prod to secure it, then prod to neaten the joint. Repeat to attach the second wing to the other side of the body.

← STEP 7 Change to a size 38 needle. Colour the forehead and back of the body with royal blue fine wool fibre, and cover the underside of the body with white fine wool fibre. The underside of the wing is half blue and half white - use a crown needle at a 45-degree angle for the wings to prevent colouring the reverse side. Continue the red down the chin and onto the breast.

→ STEP 8 Using a craft knife or small scissors, cut the beak in half and prod with a size 38 needle to neaten and refine. Use a size 36 needle to prod the eye sockets and then stitch in the glass beads securely using a doll needle and strong thread.

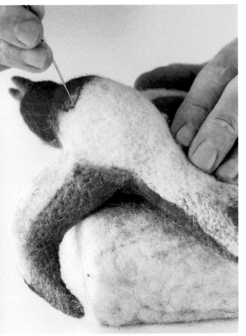
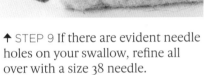

↑ STEP 9 If there are evident needle holes on your swallow, refine all over with a size 38 needle.

→ FINISHED SWALLOW Your swallow is now ready to fly.

CHICK

EQUIPMENT AND MATERIALS

- Felting block
- Needles: sizes 36, 38 and 40
- Craft knife
- Pre-felt: 20 x 30cm (8 x 12in)
- Wool fibre: 5g (⅛oz) medium in white; 25g (1oz) fine in white, sky blue, yellow, orange, black and ruby red
- For pod, see page 27

← STEP 1 Cut rectangles of pre-felt and roll them to create cylinders in the following diameter-to-length ratios: 3 : 4cm (1¼ : 1½in), 3 : 3cm (1¼ : 1¼in), (or make two wet-felted balls with diameters of 3cm (1¼in) and 4cm (1½in).

↓ STEP 2 Working against your felting block, join the cylinders together by prodding through one piece and into the other with a size 36 needle. Once the 'head' is loosely attached, keep moving the chick around and prodding to make the joint secure. Continue to prod, adding white medium wool fibre to refine the shape. Change to a size 38 needle and prod to attach one thin wisp of sky blue wool fibre at a time to the chick's back and collar. Surface the rest of the chick with white fine wool fibre. Give the head a white cap.

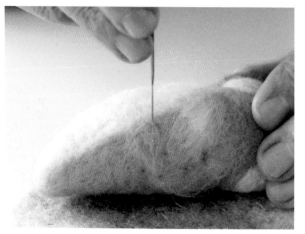

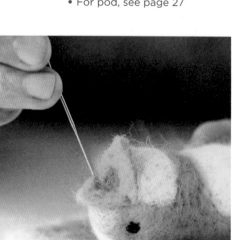

← STEP 3 The beak sits on the colour change between white and blue. To create the beak, needle felt a tiny disc of yellow, working on your felting block. Cut it into a small square, fold it diagonally and offer it up to the chick's face. Prod to attach the beak, using a tiny wisp of orange fibre. Add black eyes, positioning them within the blue band.

→ STEP 4 Add ruby red to the throat. Finish all over with a size 38 needle and then a size 40 needle, if required.

→ FINISHED CHICK Your chick is now ready to pop into a pod.

SHEEPDOG

Apparently, every historical site of human existence shows evidence of dog companions. As a dedicated dog owner, this doesn't surprise me at all.

CREATING THE SET
Needle-felted fields are set off by a stitched canvas backdrop, corrugated-cardboard shed and twig fence.

EQUIPMENT AND MATERIALS
• Felting block
• Needles: sizes 36, 38 and 40; three-needle tool (size 38)
• Craft knife; wire snips and pliers
• Pre-felt: 30 x 40cm (12 x 16in)
• Wool fibre: 50g (2oz) medium in white; 25g (1oz) fine in black and white; 5g (¼oz) fine in sky blue
• Medium craft wire: for the legs, 1 x 20cm (8in) long and 1 x 26cm (10¼in) long; for the tail, 1 x 15cm (6in) long (see pages 34 and 36)

↑ STEP 1 Make pre-felt cylinders in the following diameter-to-length ratios: body 4 : 12cm (1½ : 4¾in); head 1.5 : 4cm (⅝ : 1½in), neck 1.5 : 2cm (⅝ : ¾in). Working against your felting block, join the head and neck by prodding through one cylinder into the other with a size 36 needle, adding a little white medium wool fibre, as necessary, to create a secure joint. For the legs, referring to page 36, wrap the two lengths of wire in yarn and make two adjustable bends, as shown. For the tail, twist the wire to create a loop and stalk. Wind black wool around the stalk, covering the sharp ends, and prod to secure.

← STEP 2 Offer up the shorter wire legs to one end of the body cylinder, place a strip of pre-felt over the wire and prod to attach it loosely. Consider the legs-to-body proportions and move the wire up or down accordingly. Prod to attach it more securely. Loosely attach the longer legs to the other end of the body. Stand the body up and alter individual leg lengths, as necessary, then prod to attach the legs firmly.

← STEP 3 Thinking about the desired shape, wrap medium wool fibre around each leg, securing it by prodding into the body at the start and finish of each leg. The back legs have much larger thighs than the front legs, which remain quite thin.

↓ STEP 4 Using a three-needle tool with size 38 needles, cover the back of the body with fine black wool. Collies have quite a deep chest and a slim waist, so prod to achieve shrinkage under the tummy area. Change to a single size 38 needle and continue to cover the back legs with fine black wool.

← STEP 5 My collie Murphy had white tips, so I added fine white wool to three feet and the tail, prodding to attach it firmly.

→ STEP 6 Consider the proportions of the neck and head alongside the body and ensure they work well together. If the head needs adjusting, prod to shrink it or add more medium wool fibre to increase its size. Once you are happy with the general proportions, start defining the head itself. Shape a narrow, long nose with a pronounced forehead.

→ STEP 8 Change to a size 36 needle. Position the neck on the body and, adding medium wool fibre, as necessary, prod to secure it. Then neaten the joint with white fine fibre and a size 38 needle. Cut a slit in the rear and insert the tail loop; squeeze the felt closed and prod to secure.

← STEP 7 Cover the head and neck with fine wool fibre, adding the characteristic white stripe down the nose and black patches over the eyes, which are outlined in white. Make a black nose and mouth.

← STEP 9 Pull some staples (strands) of white fine wool off the roving and offer it up to the shoulder area, allowing the staples to lie in the same direction as dog hair. Prod across the centre of this wool fibre at right angles to the staples. Fold the wool fibre back on itself and prod again to join it securely to the body. Continue working up to the neck in this way to create a long coat.

→ FINISHED SHEEPDOG Using sky blue fine fibre and a size 40 needle, fill in the eyes and add black pupils; your sheepdog is ready to herd.

COTSWOLD SHEEP

This gorgeous sheep is a favourite project in my tutorials. As a young adult, one of my chores was to go out every night and check on the sheep newly arrived from the Welsh mountains. Few rural pleasures meet the joy of seeing lambs prance among the daffodils.

CREATING THE SET

A yarn-wound wire tree is dramatic in front of the Tussah silk backdrop. The rocks and moss are real.

EQUIPMENT AND MATERIALS

- Felting block
- Needles: sizes 36, 38 and 40
- Scissors; wire snips and pliers
- Pre-felt: 30 x 40cm (12 x 16in)
- Wool fibre: 50g (2oz) medium in white; 20g (1oz) white curly fleece; 5g (¼oz) fine in pink, yellow, black and tan
- Two lengths of medium craft wire for the legs: 30cm (12in) long (see Wirework on pages 34 and 36)

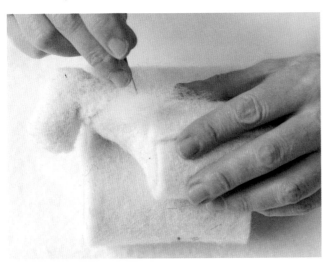

↑ STEP 1 Make all the component parts. First make three pre-felt cylinders for the body, head and neck in the following diameter-to-length ratios: body 5 : 10cm (2 : 4in); head 2 : 5cm (¾ : 2in); neck 2 : 5cm (¾ : 2in). Lay out the cylinders as shown and cut a right angle out of the neck section to help it fit better when positioned against the body section. For the legs, cover both lengths of wire with yarn and create adjustable bends (see page 36 and step 1 on page 66).

← STEP 2 Using a size 36 needle and tiny wisps of medium wool fibre, attach the neck to the body and the head to the neck, prodding to secure the joints.

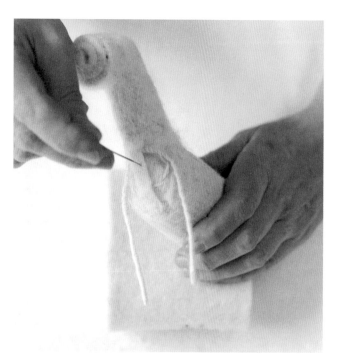

← STEP 3 Attach the front legs to the chest area using medium wool fibre or small strips of pre-felt (see also step 2 on page 66).

↓ STEP 4 Attach the back legs to the rear of the body in the same way. Adjust the lengths of the legs to enable the sheep to stand up, and prod to secure.

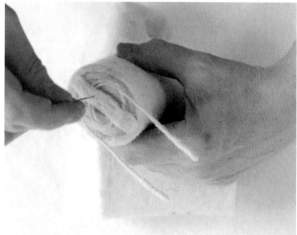

← STEP 5 Attach some lengths of medium wool fibres to the body just above the legs. Wind the fibres up and down each leg to create some shape, building up the volume at the thigh for a tapered effect. Secure the fibres back into the body and prod all over to tighten and refine.

→ STEP 6 Bend the back legs at the knee and bend all the legs at the ankle to create feet, then stand the sheep up. Build up the chest with medium wool fibre and then refine the shape all over.

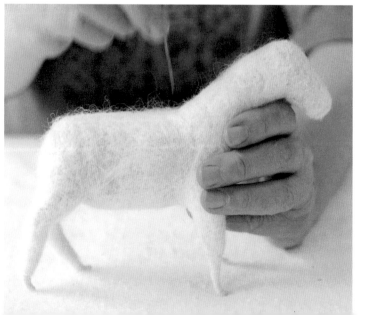

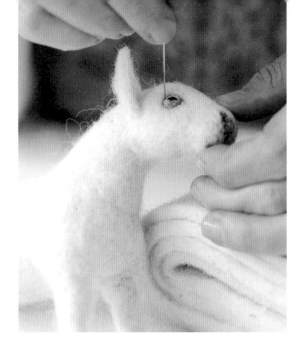

STEP 7 Use size 38 and 40 needles to create the sheep's face, prodding to sculpt the nose area with a narrow jaw coming forwards. Add a pink nose with black nostrils and a yellow eye with a black rectangular pupil. Make the ears from white fine fibre, using the 'pancake' method on page 25, and prod to attach them wide apart and far back on the head. Build a strong brow with medium fibre.

→ STEP 8 Tease small strands of curly fleece apart to create pieces 3-5mm (⅛-¼in) thick and 5cm (2in) long. Attach the cut end of each strand to the body to allow the length to fall downwards, covering the sheep's torso. Add more strands, working up the torso so each new attachment covers the last. Work in this way until the whole body is covered.

→ FINISHED SHEEP Horns are optional (depending on the breed). I chose to add tan-coloured horns, made with the 'pancake' method (see page 25), and positioned them on top of the head, between the ears.

RABBIT

Where Scottish fields reach down to the sea, there is always a strip of land seemingly owned by the wild rabbits – hundreds of undeniably cute rabbits.

CREATING THE SET

A papier-mâché (paper-pulp) field is pierced with pom-pom dandelions (see page 43). Simple felt circles are stitched onto cotton fabric for the backdrop.

EQUIPMENT AND MATERIALS

- Felting block
- Needles: sizes 36, 38 and 40; three-needle tool (size 38)
- Scissors; doll needle and strong thread
- Pre-felt: 30 x 40cm (12 x 16in)
- Wool fibre: 100g (4oz) medium in white; 25g (1oz) fine in white, pink, light and mid grey, black and brown
- Two black glass beads for eyes

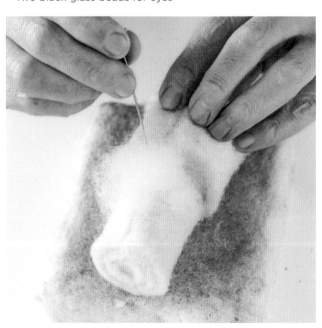

↑ STEP 1 For the body and legs, cut and roll pre-felt rectangles to create cylinders with the following diameter-to-length ratios: lower body 7 : 7cm (2¾ : 2¾in); upper body 5 : 7cm (2 : 2¾in); two hind legs 1.5 : 2cm (⅝ : ¾in); two forelegs 1.5 : 4cm (⅝ : 1½in). For the head, make a pre-felt ball 4cm (1½in) in diameter.

← STEP 2 Place the torso parts together and prod with a size 36 needle to join them, prodding wisps of medium wool fibre, as necessary, into the lower body and then the upper body until firmly secured.

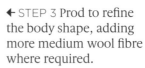

← STEP 3 Prod to refine the body shape, adding more medium wool fibre where required.

→ STEP 4 Prod to attach the two rear legs to the lower torso, helping the model to stand up. Flatten the base by prodding, then prod to attach the forelegs at the shoulders, using medium wool fibre, as necessary.

← STEP 5 Attach a small amount of medium wool fibre to the head ball to act as a neck and to hold as you work at refining the head. Create two eye sockets big enough to receive your glass beads. Build up the cheeks by repeatedly adding small wisps of fine white wool fibre.

→ STEP 6 Change to a size 38 needle to add the facial details. Prod a little pink nose in the centre of the face. Add wisps of grey to the forehead and cover in colour, following an imagined line between the snout and eye area. Add a black line for the mouth. Stitch the glass beads into the eye sockets using a doll needle and thread, working the stitches between the eyes and through to the back of the head.

→ STEP 7 For the ears, make two 'pancakes' of grey wool fibre on your felting block (see page 25), concentrating your prodding in the centre of each shape and using a three-needle tool with size 38 needles. Fold each 'pancake' in half. Prod and fold it again into quarters. Prod and fold again into an eighth of the original 'pancake'. The edge of the ear (the perimeter of the original 'pancake') should be less prodded and therefore fluffy. This area can be held safely while prodding and it also helps you attach the finished ear to the head. Give each ear a white centre.

↓ STEP 8 Offer up the first ear to the head and prod-attach with a size 38 needle. Repeat for the other ear.

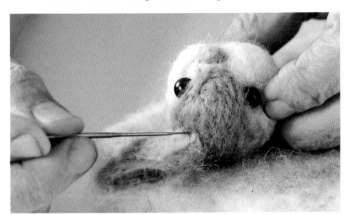

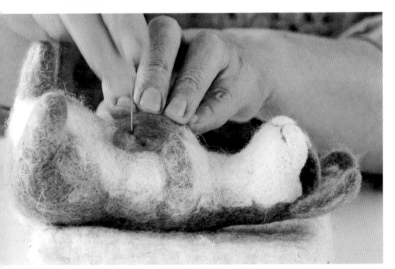

↑ STEP 9 Apply colour to the body, giving the rabbit brown paws, blending up to white and then grey. Thin layers of wool are easier to blend. Make a small ball tail from white fine fibre and prod to attach it in place on the rabbit's rear.

→ FINISHED RABBIT Your little rabbit now needs some friends. About 60 of them.

POLAR REGIONS

There is something magical about waking up to new snow. The animals that live in snowscapes are truly remarkable and exhibit incredible ways of dealing with the harsh conditions, taking fur and feathers into another realm completely. These creatures have our admiration, and here I have chosen three that are universally adored.

POLAR BEAR

This amazing animal is a great first project and is particularly good for children to make. With no wire to consider, the risk of needle breakages is minimal, and just a few simple techniques result in an adorable bear.

CREATING THE SET
A papier-mâché (paper-pulp) hill sits in front of a rag-rug backdrop.

EQUIPMENT AND MATERIALS
- Felting block
- Needles: sizes 36 and 38
- Scissors
- Pre-felt: 30 x 40cm (12 x 16in)
- Wool fibre: 50g (2oz) medium in white;
  5g (¼oz) fine in black and white

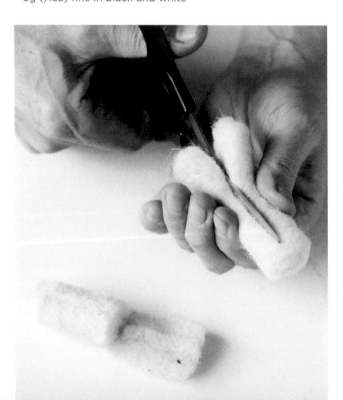

↑ STEP 1 Roll strips of pre-felt to make seven cylinders with the following diameter-to-length ratios: body 8 : 14cm (3 : 5½in); 4 x legs 3 : 13cm (1¼ : 5in); neck 3 : 5cm (1¼ : 2in); nose 2 : 3cm (¾ : 1¼in).

← STEP 2 Using scissors, cut each leg in half lengthways to halfway down and remove one section.

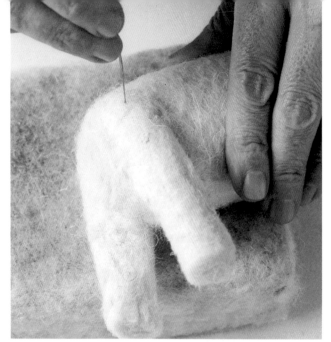

◀ STEP 3 Offer up the cut-away section of one leg to one end of the body cylinder and prod repeatedly through both pieces with a size 36 needle to attach the leg. Offer up wisps of white medium fibre to the area and continue to prod until the joint is secure. Repeat with the other legs.

↓ STEP 4 Using the same method, attach the head to the neck. Prod to shrink and refine the snout area.

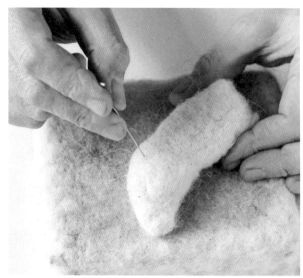

◀ STEP 5 Offer up the head and neck to the body and prod to attach, adding wisps of white medium fibre and prodding to secure the joint.

➔ STEP 6 Change to a size 38 needle. Prod all over the bear, attaching white fine fibre and refining the shape. Then add the details. Make two small ears using the 'pancake' method (see page 25). Fold one tiny 'pancake' in half to create a semicircle. Offer it up to the head and carefully prod the straight edge of the semicircle onto the head in a tight curve. Attach the other ear in the same way. Prod tiny wisps of black onto the face to create the nose, mouth and eyes. Then make five claws on each foot. Repeatedly add wisps of white fine fibre to make a short tail.

➔ ➔ FINISHED POLAR BEAR Your cuddly-looking polar bear is all set to hunt the icy waters for fish.

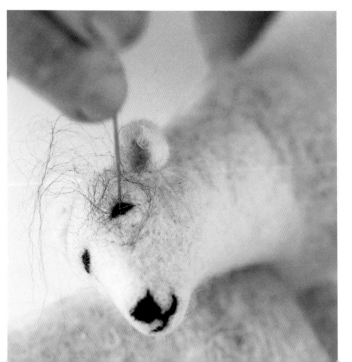

REINDEER

Not only do reindeer circumnavigate the globe in a single night, but they also spend the rest of the year in the tundra eking out an existence from lichen.

CREATING THE SET

Dye sources including rust and onion skins were used to make the backdrop and base panel (see page 45). There is a stitched silk pool and a papier-mâché (paper-pulp) cliff face.

EQUIPMENT AND MATERIALS

- Felting block
- Needles: sizes 36, 38 and 40; three-needle tool (size 38)
- Scissors or craft knife
- Wire snips and pliers
- Doll needle and strong thread
- Pre-felt: 30 x 40cm (12 x 16in)
- Wool fibre: 25g (1oz) medium in white; 10g (½oz) fine in white, two shades of grey, black and tan
- Wire: 60cm (24in) medium for the legs (see page 36); 1m (1yd) fine for the antlers (see page 37)
- 2 small black glass beads for the eyes

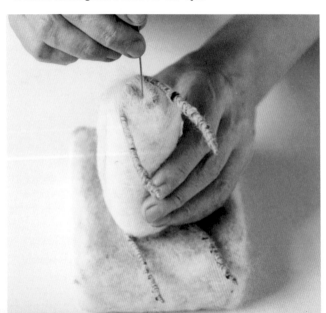

↑ STEP 1 Cut and roll rectangles of pre-felt to make three cylinders with the following diameter-to-length ratios: body 4 : 9cm (1½ : 3½in); neck 1.5 : 4cm (⅝ : 1½in); head 1.5 : 1.5cm (⅝ : ⅝in). Referring to Wirework on pages 34, cut two lengths of wire for the legs: 20cm (8in) and 26cm (10¼in). Bend the cut ends in and wrap the wires with grey yarn. Bend the shorter wire into a U-shape and make an adjustable bend in the longer wire, as shown (see page 36).

← STEP 2 Using a size 36 needle, loosely attach the shorter wire legs to one end of the body cylinder by prodding a small strip of pre-felt over the wire. Attach the longer legs to the rear. Adjust the leg lengths, as necessary. Then prod the pre-felt covering the wire to secure the legs firmly in place.

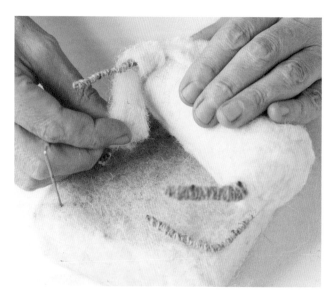

← STEP 3 Wrap small strips of pre-felt around the top of each leg to give shape to the thigh area. Prod carefully, avoiding the wire, to attach wool to wool. Wrap the legs a second time with grey fine wool fibre and prod to secure it. As you work, keep moving the leg into different positions to access different parts of it. Bend the legs to create knees and broaden them by adding wisps of wool fibre.

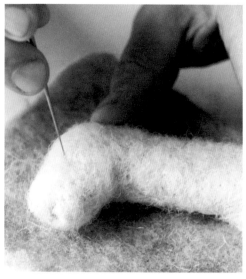

← STEP 4 Using a three-needle tool with size 38 needles, refine the body shape and cover the back and sides with a mix of grey fine wool fibres. Build up the tummy area and cover it with white fine wool fibre.

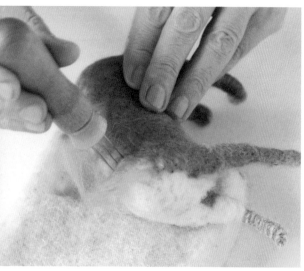

↑ STEP 5 Join the head to the neck and attach by prodding with a size 36 needle. Refine by prodding and adding medium wool fibre where you need to build up the shape.

→ STEP 6 Once you are happy with the shape of the head, change to a size 38 needle and cover it with the mix of grey fine wool fibres. Carefully cut into the muzzle with scissors, splitting it to create a mouth. Prod inside the mouth to neaten and refine it.

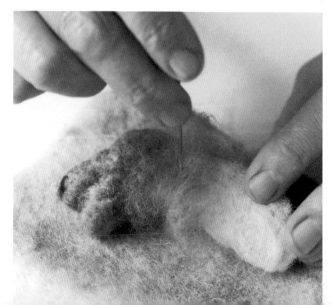

→ STEP 7 Make the eye sockets by prodding with a size 36 needle. Insert the eye beads and use a doll needle and strong thread to stitch them securely in place, stitching from eye to eye and to the underside of the chin. Change to a size 38 needle to build up the grey area around the eyes and add white eyelids. Add a black nose by prodding with black fine fibre. Make two small ears from semicircles of grey fine fibre prodded into a disc and then folded (see page 25). Position the ears, allowing space for the antlers, and prod-attach them to the head.

↑ STEP 8 For the antlers, twist two lengths of fine wire into the basic antler shape, referring to page 37. You can make them simple, if you are new to wirework, or more complicated. Create a loop at one end of each antler to insert into the reindeer's head and make sure all cut ends are bent inwards. Wind tan fine wool fibre tightly around the twisted wire. Prod carefully to secure, avoiding the wire and attaching wool to wool. Cut a slit in the top of the reindeer's head and push the wire loop into it. Squeeze the cut closed and prod repeatedly until the wire structure is held firmly.

→ FINISHED REINDEER Young reindeer have very simple horns while dominant males display huge antlers.

PENGUIN

These adorable creatures are deservedly the stars of many films and documentaries. The simple shape of the baby penguin makes it an ideal introductory project that is easy to achieve in a few hours. Individual characteristics can be added as confidence builds.

CREATING THE SET
The backdrop is Tussah silk with real rocks and a covering of artificial snow in the foreground.

EQUIPMENT AND MATERIALS
• Felting block
• Needles: sizes 36, 38 and 40
• Doll needle and strong thread
• Pre-felt: 30 x 40cm (12 x 16in)
• Wool fibre: 10g (½oz) medium in white; 5g (¼oz) fine in white, black, grey, yellow and orange
• 2 glass beads for the eyes

↑ STEP 1 Make two pre-felt balls with the following diameters: body 7cm (2¾in) and head 3cm (1¼in). Offer up a wisp of medium wool fibre to each ball and prod to attach it using a size 36 needle.

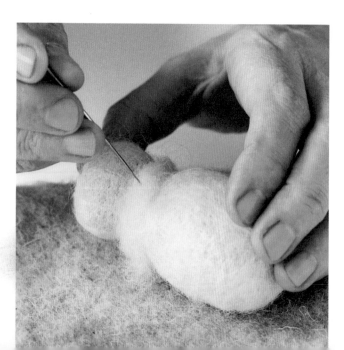

← STEP 2 Hold the balls together with the medium fibre sandwiched between them and prod through the loose wisps, first into the body and then into the head, until you have a firm joint. Strengthen and refine the joint by adding more medium wool fibre and prodding alternately into the body and head.

← STEP 3 Refine the model into a penguin shape by adding more medium fibre where you need the body to grow and prodding where you need it to shrink.

↓ STEP 4 Change to a size 38 needle to refine the penguin's face, building up cute cheeks by adding wisps of white fine wool fibre and prodding to attach and shape.

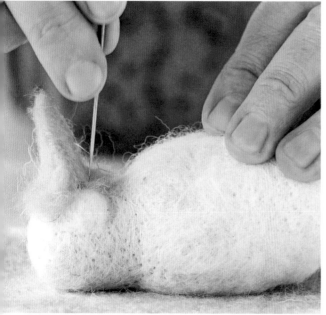

← STEP 5 Make a beak using the 'pancake' method (see page 25). First make a flat, thin disc of yellow fine wool fibre by prodding it on your felting block. Fold the disc in half and half again, then fold that in half once more, prodding to secure. Concentrate on making the tip of the beak firm with fluff at the other end. Offer the fluffy end up to the penguin's face and prod to attach it. Neaten the joint using white fine wool fibre.

→ STEP 6 Using a size 36 needle, prod two eye sockets large enough to receive the glass eye beads.

← STEP 7 Change to a size 38 needle and cover the top of the head with black fine wool, working down to the beak.

↓ STEP 8 Using a doll needle and strong thread, stitch the eye beads securely in place. Stitch repeatedly in a triangular pattern from the back of the head and from eye to eye.

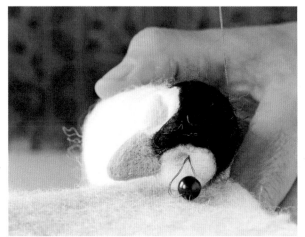

↑ STEP 9 Flatten the base of the penguin by prodding with a size 36 needle. Make two small kite-shaped feet out of orange fine wool fibre by folding up flat 'pancakes' of felt and prodding them on your felting block (see page 25). Prod to attach the feet to the base of the penguin. Add grey fine wool fibre to the body and refine with a size 38 needle, swapping to a size 40 needle, if necessary, to reduce the prod marks.

→ FINISHED PENGUIN Your penguin is now ready to receive your adoration.

UPLANDS

As a child I played daily in the hills backing onto the garden. Hours were whiled away watching the squirrels, with occasional dawn outings to spy on the badgers and foxes. The hedgehogs were more secretive, only allowing us the occasional glimpse into their lives. These creatures bring something of the wild into our projects.

GOAT

A favourite farm activity for my toddler was watching a pulley system delivering food pellets up a rocky outcrop. Little goats in the field listened out for the whirring pulley and would bounce up the rocks to claim their reward.

CREATING THE SET

Papier-mâché (paper-pulp) cliffs with knitted and felted 'grass' tops (see page 38) are placed in front of a rust-dyed backdrop (see page 45). The tree is wire and felt (see page 42).

MATERIALS AND EQUIPMENT

- Felting block
- Needles: sizes 36, 38 and 40
- Craft knife
- Wire snips and pliers
- Pre-felt: 20 x 40cm (8 x 16in)
- Wool fibre: 25g (1oz) medium in white; 5g (¼oz) fine in white, mid-brown, fawn, grey, black, pink and yellow
- Medium craft wire for the legs: 1 x 20cm (8in) long and 1 x 26cm (10¼in) long (see page 36)

↑ STEP 1 Make the component parts from pre-felt; make the cylinders from long rectangles and the ball from a tapered triangle, rolled and prodded to secure. Make two cylinders in the following diameter-to-length ratios: body 4 : 9cm (1½ : 3½in); neck: 1.5 : 4cm (⅝ : 1½in). Make a 1.5cm (⅝in) ball for the head. For the legs, referring to Wirework on page 34, cut two length of wire, 20cm (8in) and 26cm (10¼in). Fold in the sharp ends and twist them to secure, then wrap both lengths of wire with white medium wool fibre. Prod in more wool to secure with a size 36 needle.

← STEP 2 Make adjustable bends in each wire, as shown, making sure the central loops are small enough to fit onto the ends of the body cylinder.

← STEP 3 Altering the adjustable bend in the wire allows you to lengthen or shorten the legs as necessary. When you are happy with the proportions, offer up the first wire bend to the front end of the body and loosely attach it by prodding medium fibre over the loop. Repeat to attach the hind legs loosely to the other end of the body. Stand the model up and double-check the leg lengths before securing them firmly in place with more prodding.

→ STEP 4 Offer up the neck cylinder to the head and prod through one into the other, adding tiny wisps of medium fibre. Keep prodding until they are firmly attached to each other and then prod to refine the shape of the head and neck. Use the edge of the felting block to enable your prodding hand to stay as close to vertical as possible. Add white fine fibre to build a nose.

← STEP 5 Change to a size 38 needle and cover the back of the head in fawn fine fibre. Next, make the ears. Following the 'pancake' method on page 25, make two semicircles of grey fine fibre slightly larger than you want the finished ears to be, to allow for shrinkage. Fold each semicircle in half on your felting block and prod along the fold to create an ear shape. Offer up a shaped ear to one side of the head and prod to attach, then repeat with the second ear. The more you prod, the smaller and firmer the ears will become.

← STEP 6 Add the eyes. First prod a small black circle, add a yellow circle on top and prod a black pupil in the centre. Add a little pink nose and a smiling black mouth.

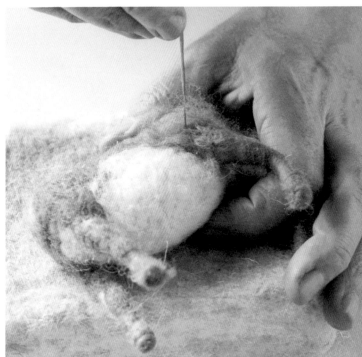

→ STEP 7 Wrap white fine wool fibre around each leg to give shape to the thigh area, the knees and the hocks, and bend the legs to create knees. Prod carefully into the wool, avoiding the wire and attaching the wool to wool. As you work on each leg, keep moving your model to access different parts. Prod until the wool is tight and secure, then work on the areas where the legs join the body. Pieces of pre-felt may help you here or you could carry on adding medium wool fibre. When you are happy with the shape, add brown fine wool to the back and legs.

Change to a size 36 needle to attach the head to the body. First add wisps of medium wool fibre to the base of the neck, to create a shape that can be offered up to the goat's body, then prod to attach. Refine all over with a size 38 and then a size 40 needle.

Using a size 38 needle, make a tail by prodding wisps of brown fine fibre securely into position on the rear.

→ FINISHED GOAT Your little goat is ready to trot off across the hillside.

FOX

I can't help admiring the fox and regularly see him in cities as well as in fields. This project includes a wire structure to add strength to your model, and the same simple method can be used for most four-legged animals.

CREATING THE SET
Stubble fields are represented with sheer fabric stitched onto felt batting and an *arashi* cotton backdrop (see page 45). Needle-felted trees complete the set (see page 42).

EQUIPMENT AND MATERIALS
• Felting block
• Needles: sizes 36 and 38
• Craft knife
• Wire snips and pliers
• Pre-felt: 20 x 40cm (8 x 16in)
• Wool fibre: 50g (2oz) medium in white; 10g (½oz) fine in fox red, white, black and yellow
• Medium craft wire for the legs and tail: 1m (1yd) (refer to Wirework on page 34)

↑ STEP 1 Make pre-felt cylinders in the following diameter-to-length ratios: body 4 : 9cm (1½ : 3½in); neck 1.5 : 4cm (⅝ : 1½in); head 1.5 : 1.5cm (⅝ : ⅝in). For the legs, cut two pieces of wire, 20cm (8in) and 26cm (10¼in). Create adjustable bends, as shown, by folding in and twisting the cut ends to secure them and then creating a loop in the middle of each wire. Wrap the wire legs in white medium fibre (see page 36).

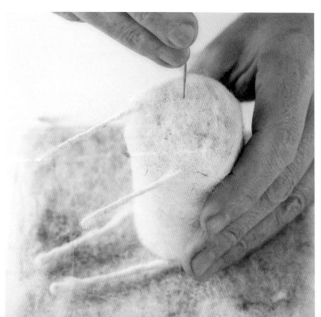

← STEP 2 With the loop in the centre, offer up the shorter legs to the front of the body. Using a size 36 needle, prod a strip of pre-felt or fibre over the wire to loosely attach it. Check the legs are in proportion with the body before attaching them firmly. Repeat this for the rear legs and bend them to create knees. Stand the model up, check the leg lengths again and prod more fibre over the wire loops to secure them.

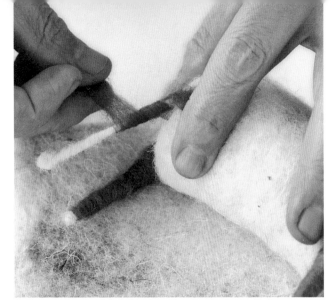

← STEP 3 Wrap fox-red fine wool fibre around each leg and, using the felting block and a size 38 needle, secure by prodding the fibre into itself.

↓ STEP 4 Build up the thighs on the rear legs, leaving the forelegs thinner. Then continue to cover the back of the fox with the red fine wool fibre.

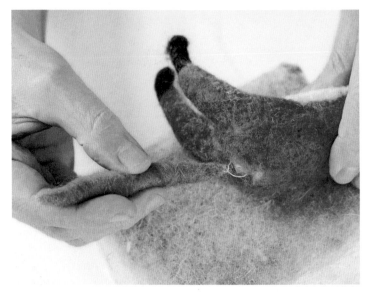

↑ STEP 5 Add black socks by winding black fine wool fibre around the bottom of the fox's legs and prodding it to secure.

→ STEP 6 To make a tail, take a 15cm (6in) length of wire, bend a loop near the middle and twist to secure. Bend the cut ends back to make the tail about 7cm (2¾in) long and ensure they are twisted securely at the fattest part of the tail. Wind red fine fibre around the wire, leaving the loop clear, and prod to tighten and secure. Cut a hole in the rear of the fox to receive the tail loop. Close the cut over the loop and prod to secure, then neaten with a little extra red fibre.

← STEP 7 Working against the felting block, attach the head to the neck at a right angle. Prod to refine the shape, adding medium white wool fibre as required. Then add red fine fibre to the snout and down the back of the neck, and add white fine fibre to the throat and cheeks.

→ STEP 8 Prod a tiny wisp of red fine wool into a 'pancake' shape and, with repeated folding and prodding, make a pair of small triangles for the ears (see page 25). Remember, they need to be sufficiently large to allow for shrinkage. Offer up the triangular ear to the head on a slight curve and very slowly and carefully prod to attach. Repeat for the second ear. Add the facial details in fine fibre: prod a triangular black nose with a black mouth, and yellow eyes with black pupils.

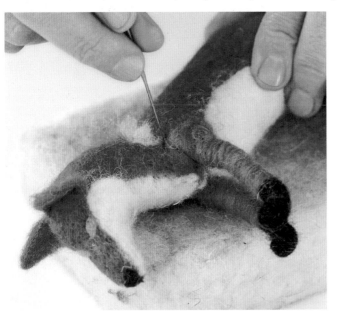

↑ STEP 9 Offer up the neck and head to the body, adding wisps of medium fibre to both pieces as 'glue'. Using a size 36 needle, prod them together until they are firmly attached. Use a size 38 needle to refine the shape and colour with red and white fine fibre.

→ FINISHED FOX Your sly old fox is ready to trot off on the hunt for hens.

HEDGEHOG

Beatrix Potter's Mrs Tiggy-Winkle is a family favourite so we have to make space for a hedgehog in our lives. This project required the purchase of specialist 'hedgehog' fabric sourced online.

CREATING THE SET
The hedgehog is in front of hand-painted papier-mâché (paper-pulp) logs with real pine cones and sycamore seeds scattered on Tussah silk.

EQUIPMENT AND MATERIALS
• Felting block
• Needles: sizes 36, 38 and 40
• Scissors
• Sewing pins
• Fabric pen or pencil
• Doll needle and strong thread
• 'Hedgehog' fabric 12 x 12cm (5 x 5in)
• Plain 'scrap' felt fabric to create a template
• Pre-felt: 40 x 20cm (16 x 8cm)
• Wool fibre: 10g (½oz) medium in white; 5g (¼oz) fine in grey, brown, fawn and white
• Two small black glass beads for the eyes

↑ STEP 1 Make the component parts as follows. For the body, roll a rectangular piece of pre-felt into a cylinder 5cm (2in) in diameter and 7cm long (2¾in). For the head, cut a long tapered triangle of pre-felt and roll it up, starting at the fat end, to create a cone about 5cm (2in) long, with a diameter of about 5cm (2in) at the fattest point. Prod to secure using a size 36 needle.

← STEP 2 Offer up the cone to the cylinder and prod to attach, using wisps of white medium wool fibre as necessary. Prod all over to refine the shape, adding more wool if required.

← STEP 3 Prod to create a definite head shape, with a gentle curve down to the nose lifting up to a strong forehead. Start to colour the nose area by adding in very thin wisps of randomly aligned fine wool in a mix of grey, brown and fawn. Create a blended brown surface using a size 38 needle.

← STEP 4 Using the 'pancake' method described on page 25, create two tiny cheeks in white fine wool fibre, and prod to attach one to each side of the face, checking from the front that they match and are level.

← STEP 5 From your scrap felt, cut an oval 12cm (5in) long and 10cm (4in) wide; fold the felt in half lengthways before you cut the oval to ensure it is symmetrical. Offer up this fabric to the hedgehog's body to try it out for size. It needs to reach from the top of the forehead to the base of the bottom and to cover the sides completely. At this stage, don't worry about making darts (see step 6) – you just need to make sure the fabric spans your hedgehog's body. Trim down the length and width as necessary. Using the scrap felt as a template, cut the same shape out of the 'hedgehog' fabric.

→ STEP 6 Using the scrap template again, position it over the hedgehog's body and pin it at the forehead, bottom and sides. This will help you to see the excess fabric. Pinch the fabric together to consider where the darts should be: you will need one above the bottom and one above each ear area. Pin the darts and check over the body again to ensure the fabric fits. Cut away the excess of each dart, allowing 1mm (¹⁄₁₀in) as an overlap on each edge.

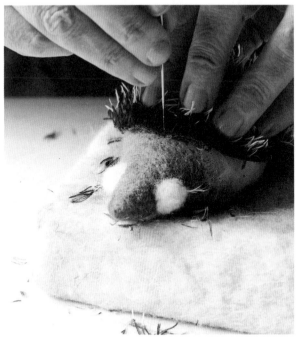

← STEP 7 Once you are sure the template fits, copy and cut three equivalent darts into the 'hedgehog' fabric.

↑ STEP 8 Offer up the 'hedgehog' fabric to the body and pin it in place. To attach the cut edges, place the tiniest wisp of black wool fibre on top, and prod through the fabric and into the body to secure it. Work all around the cut edge in this way.

↑ STEP 9 Place a pin where you want each eye to be and mark with a fabric pen or pencil, then use a size 36 needle to prod two eye sockets. Using a doll needle and strong thread, stitch a bead into each hole as you would sew on a button, stitching from one eye to the other and under the chin for extra strength. Prod white fine fibre around the beads to accentuate the eyes, using a size 38 needle and then a size 40 needle.

→ FINISHED HEDGEHOG Put your hedgehog in his woodland setting with some autumn leaves to nest under.

SNAIL

Snails are fascinating, from the strange texture and colourful skirt to the slow movements of the tentacles and the stunning whorl of the shell. This project introduces basic wirework. And once you can make one whorl, you can alter the pattern to make many more.

CREATING THE SET
The snail sits on top of a papier-mâché (paper-pulp) log with a textured *arashi* backdrop hand-stitched onto felt batting (see page 45).

EQUIPMENT AND MATERIALS
• Felting block
• Needles: sizes 36, 38 and 40
• Craft knife; wire snips and pliers
• Pre-felt: ball 3cm (1¼in) diameter
• Wool fibre: 100g (4oz) medium in white; 50g (2oz) fine in white and grey; 10g (½oz) fine in black, yellow and fawn
• Craft wire: one length of 30cm (12in) and one length of 40cm (16in) medium, for the body and shell; 30cm (12in) fine, for the tentacles

↑ STEP 1 Take the 30cm (12in) of medium wire and bend a loop at one end, twisting to secure. Thread a little medium wool through the loop and squeeze the wire to trap the fibre. Wrap the fibre down the length and prod it with a size 36 needle to prevent it from unwrapping. Repeat from the other end and keep wrapping and prodding to create a thin cylinder 15cm (6in) long, tapering from 2cm (¾in) diameter at the broader end to 1cm (½in) at the narrower end.

← STEP 2 For the tentacles, bend one cut end of the fine wire back on itself and twist to secure, creating a small loop. Allowing for each tentacle to be 1cm (½in) and for the wire to span the top of the head, snip the wire to length and create a loop at the other end.

STEP 3 Change to a size 38 needle. Thread a wisp of black fine wool fibre through each loop and prod to attach it to itself, squeezing the loop to trap the fibre securely. Wrap grey fine fibre around the wire in between the black looped ends and prod to secure.

STEP 4 Attach the head to the body using a size 36 needle, offering up wisps of medium fibre to the fatter end of the cylinder and the pre-felt ball and prodding the pieces together and refining the shape.

STEP 5 Resurface the snail's body with grey fine wool fibre using a size 36 needle first and then a size 38 needle. Add more grey fibre to broaden out the 'skirt' area of the snail.

STEP 6 Cut open the top of the head and insert the grey part of the tentacles, with the telescopic eyes poking out of the snail's forehead. Check the position of the tentacles and make sure they are the same height. When you are happy, squeeze the cut shut and prod to close it back together. Add extra grey fibre to refine the surface.

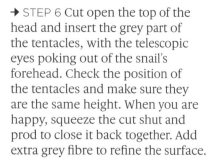

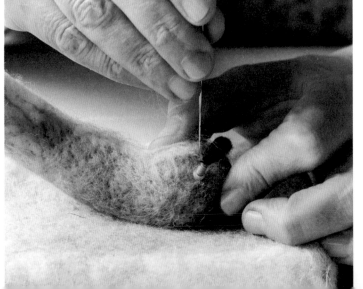

↑ STEP 7 Change to a size 38 needle and cover the head and body with elongated twizzle-bumps (see also steps 5-7 on pages 130-1). Offering up a wisp of white fine fibre to the surface, push the needle into the snail and repeatedly lift and prod, without taking the needle out of the body, until the wisp is attached. Then take the needle out and, making tiny circles in a 'twizzle' motion, surround the needle with fibre and prod-attach a raised bump.

↑ STEP 8 To make the shell, take the longer length of medium wire and, using a size 36 needle, cover it with white medium wool fibre in the same way as you did for the body (see step 1). Make sure the cut ends of the wire are safely twisted inwards and covered with wool. Keep winding fibres around the wire and prodding to attach them, to create a tapered cylinder that broadens rapidly over the last 15cm (6in) from 3cm (1¼in) diameter to 6cm (2⅜in) diameter. Changing to a size 38 needle, cover the narrow end with fine yellow fibres, prodding to attach them.

← STEP 9 Starting at the narrow end, wind up the cylinder to form a whorl, making an initial prod-attachment with a size 36 needle to secure the end to itself.

← STEP 10 Check the reverse of the shell shape; it should have a definite dip but you may need to broaden the fat end. When you are happy, prod to attach the curved cylinder to itself.

→ STEP 11 Using a size 38 needle, and black, grey and fawn fine wool fibres, add colour details following the spiral shape.

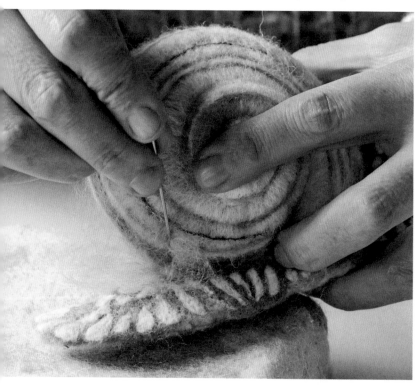

← STEP 12 Prod-attach the body to the shell, offering extra grey fibre, as necessary, to make the joint secure. Finally, add two smaller tentacles to the nose area using fine grey fibre.

→ FINISHED SNAIL Your snail is now ready to travel.

DORMOUSE

This little dormouse is a complete darling, fast asleep in her horse-chestnut case. She is one of my most popular exhibits at shows. Be prepared to put in quite a bit of time, as the charm lies all in the level of finish.

CREATING THE SET

A felt mushroom (see page 40) and a papier-mâché (paper-pulp) horse-chestnut case (see page 43) are complemented by real forest finds.

EQUIPMENT AND MATERIALS
• Felting block
• Needles: sizes 38 and 40
• Pre-felt: 20 x 10cm (8 x 4in)
• Wool fibre: 25g (1oz) fine in flesh pink, mouse brown, white and black.

↑ STEP 1 Create the component parts. Make a pre-felt ball 5cm (2in) in diameter. Cut a tiny isosceles triangle of pre-felt to help shape the head. For the legs, roll and prod, with a size 38 needle, a thin cylinder of flesh-pink fine wool fibre. Cut it into four lengths of 3cm (1¼in). For the tail, roll and prod a fatter cylinder 6cm (2⅜in) long in mouse-brown fine wool fibre.

← STEP 2 Offer up the triangle of pre-felt to the ball and prod to attach it.

← STEP 3 Cover the head with mouse-brown fine wool fibre, prodding to attach it. Continue over the back of the ball, leaving the tummy area white.

↓ STEP 4 Fatten out the cheeks using brown fine wool fibre and refine the area around the face.

← STEP 5 Attach the forelegs by prodding them into the body. Prod to refine the feet, creating three tiny toes on each.

→ STEP 6 Attach the rear legs by prodding them into the body in the same way. Prod to refine the toes and heels.

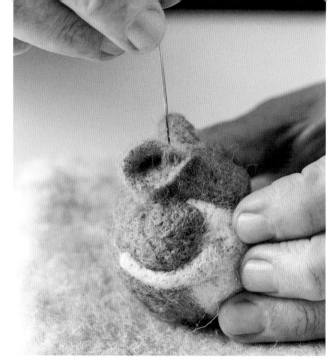

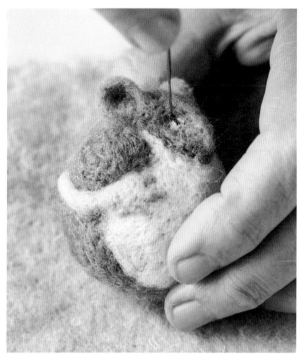

→ STEP 7 Using the 'pancake' method (see page 25) and mouse-brown fibre, make two tiny (1.5cm/⅝in diameter) semicircles for the ears. Fold and prod to form the ear shape before securing them to the head.

↑ STEP 8 Add the facial details using fine fibre and a size 38 then 40 needle. Prod tiny white circles with a central black line to make closed eyes, and a pink nose.

↑ STEP 9 Attach the tail so it curls around to the body and refine the join with mouse-brown fibre. Refine all over with a size 40 needle.

→ FINISHED DORMOUSE Make a papier-mâché (paper-pulp) horse-chestnut case (see page 43) and pop your dormouse inside so she can snooze in comfort.

RED SQUIRREL

The red squirrel is a delight to watch, rushing about gathering nuts for his winter store. This project requires patience and a range of skills: needle-felting basics, wiring legs, and creating character and details.

CREATING THE SET
A Tussah silk backdrop and needle-felted hemp base complement the papier-mâché (paper-pulp) silver birch trees finished with real birch sloughs (see page 40).

EQUIPMENT AND MATERIALS
- Felting block
- Needles: sizes 36, 38 and 40; three-needle tool (size 38)
- Craft knife
- Doll needle and strong thread
- Pre-felt: 30 x 40cm (12 x 16in)
- Wool fibre: 100g (4oz) medium in white; 50g (2oz) fine in squirrel red; 5g (⅙oz) fine in white, plum and green
- Two black glass beads, 6mm (¼in) diameter, for the eyes

↑ STEP 1 Cut and roll rectangles of pre-felt to create cylinders in the following diameter-to-length ratios: lower body 7 : 7cm (2¾ : 2¾in); upper body 5 : 7cm (2 : 2¾in); neck 1.5 : 2cm (⅝ : 1¼in); 2 forelegs 1.5 : 4cm (⅝ : 1½in); 2 hind legs 1.5 : 2cm (⅝ : ¾in). For the thighs, make 2 flat ovals 3 x 4cm (1¼ x 1½in). For the head, make a ball 4cm (1½in) in diameter. For the tail, create a 5 : 14cm (2 : 5½in) cylinder and, using a size 36 needle, add medium white fibre to shape, as shown. Join the head to the neck, and the upper body to the lower body.

← STEP 2 Leaving the belly, chest and face white, cover the rest of the body and the other pieces with red fine wool using a three-needle tool with size 38 needles.

STEP 3 Start to assemble the component parts. Add the two rear legs at right angles to the base of the body, so the model can stand up. Flatten the base by prodding to shrink it (see page 22). Prod the thigh discs and prod to attach. Refine the shape at each stage with a size 38 needle.

STEP 4 Create a green acorn using the 'pancake' method on page 25. Attach the forelegs to it, prodding to create little toes.

STEP 5 Attach the tops of the forelegs to the shoulders using fine red wool fibre as necessary.

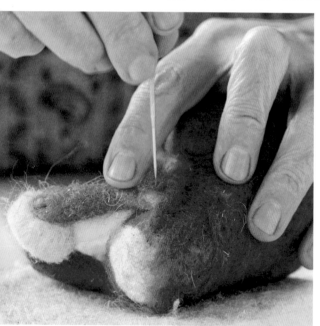

→ STEP 6 Using a size 36 needle, create two eye sockets large enough to receive your glass beads. Build up the cheeks by repeatedly adding small wisps of white fine wool fibre. Add a plum-coloured nose and mouth using a size 38 needle. Then add wisps of red fine wool fibre to the forehead and snout.

← STEP 7 Using a doll needle and strong thread, stitch the eye beads firmly in place, taking the stitches between the eyes and down to the chin repeatedly until the beads are secure.

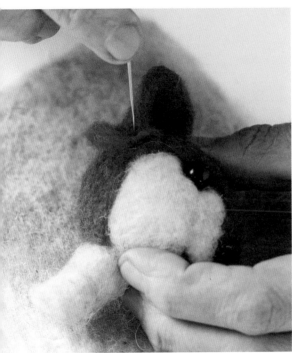

↑ STEP 8 On your felting block make two very small 'pancakes' of red fine wool (see page 25), using a size 38 needle. Fold them in half to make the ears. Prod to neaten and shrink to size. Offer up the ears to the head and prod to secure. Refine the head details with the size 38 needle and then a size 40 needle.

→ FINISHED SQUIRREL Add the bushy tail to the base of the body, prodding with a size 36 needle to attach it securely. Neaten the joint with a size 38 needle, and your squirrel is complete.

OWL

Perched on his branch, this wise old owl has more surface pattern, component parts and techniques than any other project in the book, so prepare yourself for a weekend marathon. It will be well worth the effort.

CREATING THE SET
The set is made completely from papier-mâché (paper pulp), which has then been hand-painted.

EQUIPMENT AND MATERIALS
- Felting block
- Needles: sizes 36, 38 and 40; three-needle tool (size 38)
- Craft knife or scissors; wire snips and pliers
- Pre-felt: 30 x 20cm (12 x 6½in)
- Wool fibre: 100g (4oz) medium in white; 25g (1oz) fine in brown; 10g (½oz) fine in white, yellow ochre, grey and black
- Papier-mâché (paper-pulp) eyes, 1.5m (⅝in) diameter, painted orange and black
- Medium craft wire for the legs, 1m (1yd)

↑ STEP 1 Make the component parts. For the head, make a rectangular block of pre-felt measuring 8 x 5 x 5cm (3 x 2 x 2in); for the body, use pre-felt or white medium wool fibre to make a ball 10cm (4in) in diameter. For the beak, use a size 38 needle to make a 'pancake' of yellow-ochre fine wool (see page 25). Fold and prod it until you have a thin sausage shape.

← STEP 2 Cut a brow-shaped piece of pre-felt, as shown, and offer it up to the head to build up the forehead while leaving the eye area flat. The eyes will be concave, sinking down into the sockets. Refine the head shape by prodding it with a size 36 needle and adding white medium wool fibre, as necessary, to create a gentle curve at the back and a flat top.

← STEP 3 Using a three-needle tool with size 38 needles, continue to refine the shape of the head and eye sockets. Then add yellow-ochre fine wool fibre to the back of the head, the forehead and the beak area.

↓ STEP 4 Offer up the beak to the front of the head and check the proportions. Adjust as necessary and then prod with a size 36 needle to attach it securely between the eye sockets.

← STEP 5 Using the three-needle tool, refine the body into more of an egg shape, by lengthening it downwards and backwards towards the tail. Keep comparing it to the head to maintain the correct proportions. Add yellow-ochre fine wool to the back, following an imagined line from the shoulder to the tail.

→ STEP 6 Using a size 36 needle and yellow-ochre fine wool fibre, make a series of three discs for each wing (see pages 24–5). The largest disc will have a smoothly curved top edge and a four-'feathered' fluted bottom edge. The second disc will have a three-'feathered' fluted bottom edge and the third disc will be smooth. Each wing is made up of three discs.

← STEP 7 Change to a size 38 needle to create the wing pattern, using white and grey fine wool fibre to make a series of white circles with grey detailing on each wing disc (see Adding colour, page 28).

↑ STEP 8 Turn the wing discs over and prod-attach them to each other. If this creates small dots on the right side, neaten by making shallow prods with the needle held at a 45-degree angle.

↑ STEP 9 Change to a size 36 needle and attach the top of one wing to one of the shoulders, adding more white medium fibre as required to secure it. Repeat to attach the second wing.

→ STEP 10 Hold the head in position on the body and, using medium white fibre as 'glue', prod from one to the other to attach. Continue until secure, and neaten the joint with first medium and then fine fibre.

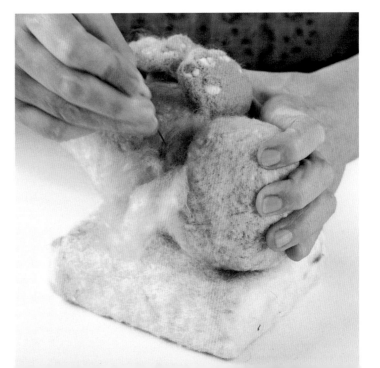

← STEP 11 Referring to the Wirework section on page 34, create a wire structure to support the owl using medium wire. Shape the wire, starting at the top of one leg and working down to the foot. Bend the wire into the first toe shape using pliers. Repeat for three more toes. Return up the leg, across the underbelly in a semicircle and to the top of the second leg. Create the second leg to match the first, finishing with another semicircle to complete the circle that will sit inside the owl's body. Bind extra wire around this circle to help attachment.

→ STEP 12 Offer up the leg structure to the body to help you decide where the support hoop should be inserted, checking how long the legs will be. Use a craft knife or scissors to cut through the belly so that you can insert the support hoop far enough to position the legs on either side of the body. Squeeze the cut in the belly closed over the wire and prod to secure it. Neaten the area with white fine wool fibre and a size 36 needle, then a size 38 needle.

← STEP 13 Cover the external wire first with white medium wool fibre, then fine wool fibre, prodding with a size 38 needle to attach it to itself and to tighten it. Add wisps of black fine wool fibre to the tips of each 'toe' to make talons.

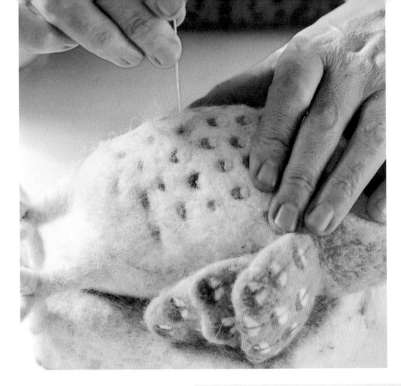

← STEP 14 Prod eye sockets with a size 36 needle and insert the papier-mâché (paper-pulp) eyeballs. Rebuild the eye area around the eyeballs to keep them in place and finish by adding 'eyebrow' details with a size 38 needle. Using the same needle, prod small circles of white fine wool fibre into the front of the owl and add detail with grey fine fibre. If required, finish off with a size 40 needle.

→ FINISHED OWL
Your wise old owl is ready to sit up on his perch.

COAST

My childhood summers spent on Devonshire beaches inspired a lifelong hankering for the coast. This was an impulse I readily submitted to, raising my own child on the west coast of Scotland. Oystercatchers (or 'sea-pies') and gulls were our daily companions as we wandered along the beaches pretending to be pirates, or climbed rocky outcrops and clifftops attempting to photograph nesting birds. I can't think of anything with a greater power of rejuvenation than the tides.

STARFISH

Others head to the Highland Show for the Scottish dancing and the whisky, but for me, the marine biologists' marquee with its stunning array of live starfish is the main attraction. This very easy project introduces some great skills, including the 'twizzle-bump'.

CREATING THE SET

The sand is an *arashi* panel, dyed using onion skins, stitched onto felt batting (see page 45). The pebbles and shells are mostly felt (see page 41) with the occasional real one.

EQUIPMENT AND MATERIALS

- Felting block
- Needles: size 36; star needles sizes 36, 38 and 40; crown needle size 38
- Scissors
- Pre-felt: 30 x 40cm (12 x 16in)
- Wool fibre: 5g (¼oz) medium in white; 50g (2oz) fine in bright and pale orange; 10g (½oz) fine in bright pink and white

↑ STEP 1 Make five legs and a body from a double layer of pre-felt. Each leg is a tapered, flattened isosceles triangle, 4 x 12cm (1½ x 4¾in). The body is a disc 8cm (3in) in diameter. Using a size 36 needle, prod and refine the shapes by adding medium wool fibre.

← STEP 2 Cover the legs and body with bright orange fine wool fibre using a size 38 star needle. Prod at 45 degrees to reduce the occurrence of white dots on the underside of the starfish.

← STEP 3 Hold up each leg in turn to the central body disc, spacing them evenly, and use a size 36 star needle to prod wisps of medium white wool fibre through both components until the joints are secure.

↓ STEP 4 Using a size 38 crown needle, neaten the surface with bright orange and bright pink fine wool.

← STEP 5 Add the first twizzle-bump to one of the legs. To do this, offer up a wisp of pale orange fine wool fibre to the leg, push a size 38 star needle through the wool fibre and into the leg. Raise and drop the needle without removing it from the leg until it has firmly caught some wool fibre. Then, lifting the tip of the needle just out of the leg, spin the point in a 'twizzle' motion until it has caught the wool fibre, then push the needle back into the same hole.

→ STEP 6 Continue with the up-and-down motion until a bump has formed, then neaten the bump with the size 38 crown needle.

← STEP 7 Repeat the process in step five with a smaller wisp of white fine wool to make a smaller twizzle-bump on top of the original pale orange twizzle-bump.

↓ STEP 8 Continue decorating the legs and body with double twizzle-bumps, creating a symmetrical pattern and prodding to shrink the twizzle-bumps with a size 38 star needle.

← STEP 9 Using the tip of a size 38 and then a size 40 star needle, finish the twizzle-bumps off neatly and join them all together with a fine line of white fine wool fibre.

→ FINISHED STARFISH
Your completed starfish is now ready to brighten up your life.

SEAGULL

No beach scene is complete without the notorious gull, the cheekiest of characters. This common gull is made from just a few component parts and is easily adapted to be a nesting gull. It is a good project to introduce wirework legs, as they are not too long, so the body balance is easy to achieve.

CREATING THE SET

Papier-mâché (paper-pulp) cliffs are topped with knitted grass (see page 38). The backdrop is an *arashi* cotton, dyed with onion skins and rust, and the sea is a patchwork of silk sari offcuts (see page 45).

EQUIPMENT AND MATERIALS

- Felting block
- Needles: sizes 36, 38 and 40
- Scissors
- Wire snips and pliers
- Pre-felt: 30 x 40cm (12 x 16in)
- Wool fibre: 50g (2oz) medium in white; 10g (½oz) fine in grey and white; 5g (¼oz) fine in red, yellow and black
- Hand-made papier-mâché (paper-pulp) eyes or commercial eyes, 1cm (⅜in) diameter
- Medium craft wire for the legs: 1.2m (1⅓yd)

↑ STEP 1 Make the component parts from pre-felt. For the head, make a ball 4cm (1½in) in diameter. For the neck, make a cylinder 1.5cm (⅝in) in diameter and 2cm (¾in) long. For the body, make a tapered, egg-shaped cylinder that is 10cm (4in) in diameter at its widest point and 14cm (5½in) long.

← STEP 2 Using a size 36 needle, prod-attach the head to the neck. Then refine the body shape, adding white medium wool fibre, as required.

STEP 3 Holding the neck, prod a large eye socket into the side of the head. Make sure it is large enough to accept the eye.

STEP 4 Insert the eyeball into the socket. Prod the area around it repeatedly, adding wisps of medium wool fibre to build up the eyelids and bringing them slightly over the eyeball to securely hold it in place. Repeat the above for the other eye.

STEP 5 Take the body and prod fine grey wool fibre onto the back, following an imaginary wing line (see Creating a neat colour change, page 29). Use black fine wool fibre to create the V-shaped detail at the tip of the tail.

STEP 6 Prod-attach the neck to the body, adding wisps of white medium wool fibre.

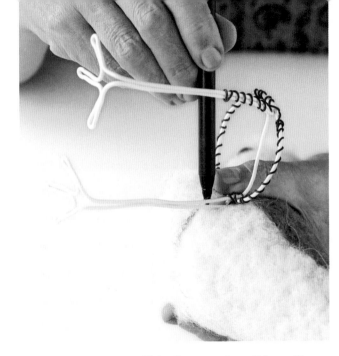

→ STEP 7 To support the gull's body some 8cm (3in) off the ground, the legs are attached to a wire circle, which is secured inside the body. This helps to counteract the natural pitching tendency of legged models (see Wirework, page 34). Referring to page 37, take 70cm (28in) of wire and, starting at the thigh, work downwards to the foot. Bend the wire to form the first toe using pliers. Repeat twice more. Return up the leg, across the underbelly of the gull and down the second leg. Repeat the foot shape and work back up the thigh, returning under the belly to the first thigh and twist to join. Take 25cm (10in) of wire and make a circle the diameter of the belly. Attach the two structures together with the remaining wire (as a visual aid, I used a different colour). Offer up the wire structure to the gull's body and mark the ideal position with a pen.

→ STEP 8 Cut off the front section of the gull's belly and place the wire structure into the cut. Replace the belly section over the wire and prod to secure. Neaten with white medium wool fibre.

← STEP 9 Prod the end of a strand of red fine wool fibre into the underbelly at the top of the first leg to secure it. Wind red fibre around the wire leg, working down to the toes and back up again. Prod the fibre to itself to attach and tighten. Repeat with second leg and fill in between the toes to create webbed feet.

← STEP 10 Change to a size 38 needle to create the beak using yellow fine wool fibre and the 'pancake' method (see page 25). Add a bright red dot at the end of the beak.

↓ STEP 11 Offer up the beak to the front of the gull's head and prod to attach. Neaten and strengthen the joint by adding white fine wool fibre.

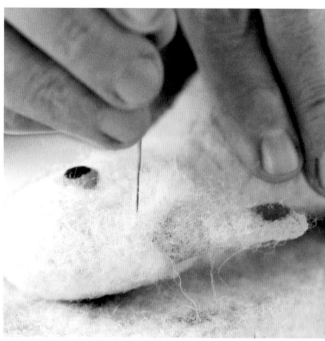

← STEP 12 Add a row of three white dots to each side of the tail tip. Refine all over with a size 38 needle and then a size 40 needle, if required.

→ FINISHED GULL Your gull is ready to perch on the clifftop, on the lookout for fishing boats.

OYSTERCATCHER

The oystercatcher is an elegant wading bird that is easy to re-create in felt. This version includes a wirework beak and legs but, like the gull, it can be made as a nesting bird. The long legs raise the centre of gravity so we add an internal stabilizing hoop.

CREATING THE SET
Arashi techniques were used for the beach-effect fabric (see page 45), which is scattered with felt pebbles and shells (see page 41).

EQUIPMENT AND MATERIALS
- Felting block
- Needles: sizes 36, 38 and 40
- Scissors or craft knife
- Wire snips and pliers
- Pre-felt: 30 x 40cm (12 x 16in)
- Wool fibre: 50g (2oz) medium in white; 25g (1oz) fine in black; 10g (½oz) fine in red and white
- Craft wire: 1m (1yd) medium for the legs; 20cm (8in) fine for the beak

↑ STEP 1 For the head and neck, make a pre-felt cylinder 4cm (1½in) in diameter and 7cm (2¾in) long. For the body, make an egg shape that is 10cm (4in) in diameter at its widest point and 14cm (5½in) long. For the beak, take 20cm (8in) of fine craft wire, fold it in half and twist to create a loop. Then fold back the cut ends and twist them back into the wire to secure. Wind red fine wool fibre over the length of the beak, leaving the loop uncovered. Carefully prod the wool into itself to tighten and secure using a size 36 needle.

← STEP 2 Build up the body, adding white medium wool fibre as required. Refine the head and neck, prodding to flatten the sides of the head.

STEP 3 Cover the entire head with black fine wool fibre, prodding to attach it.

STEP 4 To add the eyes, prod red fine wool fibre into both sides of the head, making sure the eyes are level and the same size. It is easier to place the beak centrally between the eyes than it is to prod the eyes equidistant from the beak.

STEP 5 To attach the beak, first work out the ideal position and then cut a slot in the front of the head, wide enough to fit the wire loop. Insert the beak loop, squeeze the slot closed and prod to secure it. Neaten the area by adding a little more fine black wool.

STEP 6 Attach the head to the body, prodding to neaten and refine the joint. Add a black dot to the eyes, and then refine all over, first with a size 38 and then a size 40 needle.

→ STEP 7 Referring to Wirework on pages 34-7, create a wire structure to support the oystercatcher. Using medium craft wire, start at the top of the first leg, work down to the foot and bend the wire into the first toe shape using pliers. Repeat to make another two toes. Work back up the leg, taking the wire under the belly in a semicircle and to the top of the second leg. Create the second leg to match the first, ending in another semicircle to complete the ring of wire that will sit inside the body. Offer up the wire structure to the body. Cut open the belly and push the wire structure inside. Replace the belly over the wire and prod with a size 36 needle to secure.

↑ STEP 8 Cover the wire legs by wrapping them in red fine wool fibre. Wrap white fine wool fibre around the top of the legs to make thighs. Prod to attach the wool to itself, avoiding the wire.

→ FINISHED OYSTERCATCHER Note the addition of a stabilizing hoop to anchor the oystercatcher to a block of wood.

Resources

I source my materials via three retail sectors: local shops, online retailers and wool festivals.

Local shops and online retailers increasingly stock needle-felting supplies and the range available is broadening. Below is one of my favourite suppliers, which sells a great range of wools and, unusually, carded wool batts in a lovely range of colours and textures.

World of Wool
worldofwool.co.uk

Regional wool festivals are the places to go for items that are not locally or readily available. New wool festivals are being launched every year, and attending one will reward you with a vast array of passionate and knowledgeable small traders, many of whom sell online. There are stalls I regularly visit at these shows, including Bronte Glen, Wingham Wools and John Arbon.

WOOL FESTIVALS AND TEXTILE SHOWS

UK

Country Living Fair
Twice-yearly events in Glasgow, London, Harrogate and Belfast
countrylivingfair.com

Edinburgh Yarn Festival
Edinburgh, Lothian
edinyarnfest.com

Fibre-East
Ampthill Bedfordshire
fibre-east.co.uk

Highland Wool and Textiles
Dingwall, Ross and Cromarty
highlandwoolandtextiles.co.uk

The Knitting and Stitching Show
In Dublin, Edinburgh, London and Harrogate
theknittingandstitchingshow.com

Unravel - A Festival of Knitting
Farnham, Surrey
craft.farnhammaltings.com

Wonderwool Wales
Builth Wells, Wales
wonderwoolwales.co.uk

Woolfest
Cockermouth, Cumbria
woolfest.co.uk

Yarndale
Skipton, Yorkshire
yarndale.co.uk

FRANCE

Journées Nationales de la Laine
Felletin, Creuse, Limousin
felletin-tourisme.fr

GERMANY

Leipziger Wolle-Fest & Stoffmesse
Leipziger, Saxony
leipziger-wollefest.de

Wollfest
Hamburg and Regensburg, Bavaria
wollfest-Hamburg.de

USA, CANADA AND AUSTRALIA

FiberArts.org
fiberarts.org

Fiber Events
fiberevents.com

Fiddlehead Fibers
fiddleheadfibers.com

Knitter's Review
knittersreview.com

Rocky Mountain Natural Colored Sheep Breeders Association
rmncsba.org

Textile Links
textilelinks.com

FELT ASSOCIATIONS

Canberra Region Feltmakers
Canberra, Australia
crfelters.org.au

Feltmakers Ireland
Southern Ireland
feltmakersireland.com

Feltmakers North
Northern Ireland
feltmakersnorth.blogspot.co.uk

International Feltmakers Association
Worldwide felting news and events
feltmakers.com

The Northeast Feltmakers Guild
New England, USA
northeastfeltmakersguild.org

FELTING MAGAZINES

Felt (manorhousemagazines.co.uk and pocketmags.com)

Felt Matters (feltmakers.com)

Glossary

ADJUSTABLE BEND A method of creating a loop to allow easy length adjustment. Used for creating wirework legs (see page 36).

ALPACA A South American animal of the camelid family, similar in appearance to the llama, with very strong yet fine wool fibre.

ANGORA This term refers to both a breed of rabbit and a breed of goat, both of which are used for their wool.

ANIMAL FIBRES Fibres that are taken from animals, as opposed to plants.

ARASHI A traditional *shibori* resist-dye technique (see page 45).

BATT See Wool batt.

BATTING Sheeting that was traditionally used sandwiched between finer fabrics to make quilts.

BLEND When mixed together, two or more elements (different weights or colours of fibres) are referred to as a blend.

BLENDING The process of mixing two elements (different weights or colours of fibres) together.

CARDED WOOL Wool that has been passed over turning drums surfaced with fine pins in order to clear away debris and align fibres.

CELLULOSE FIBRES Cellulose is the building block of plants; cellulose fibre is plant-based, as opposed to animal-based fibre.

COMBED WOOL Wool that has been carded and repeatedly passed over drums of pins, exhibiting very neatly aligned fibres.

FELT Fabric made of entangled and matted, rather than woven, fibres.

FELT SHEETING A non-woven fabric in sheet form.

FELTING The process of making felt.

HAND CARDERS A pair of paddles covered with a sheet of pins, sized to enable carding by hand.

KANTHA STITCH An Asian style of stitching using running stitch and layers of different fibres (traditionally sari offcuts) to create new textile pieces.

KNITTING The craft of creating a series of interlocking loops of yarn to create a loose fabric. Usually made using two long needles.

OBERON POD A felt vessel, built around a pine-cone resist, named after Fi Oberon (see page 26).

PRE-FELT (PROTO-FELT) Felt material halfway through the making process, when the fibres are gently matted together and can still be teased apart.

PROTEIN FIBRES Fibres sourced from animals, as opposed to cellulose fibres which are sourced from plants.

RAG-RUGGING A folk craft in which scraps of fabric are attached to a hessian (burlap) backing, creating a heavily textured rug.

ROVING Carded and combed wool fibres that have been passed through a tube.

SCOURING The process of cleaning a fleece.

SHIBORI A traditional and comprehensive range of resist-dye techniques, often generically referred to as 'tie-dye'.

SPINNING Combining and twisting fibres into yarn.

TWIZZLE-BUMP A technique to create a needle-felted raised bump by 'twizzling' fibre around a needle before prodding to attach (see steps 5-7 on pages 130-1).

WET FELTING Soaking fibre and agitating it with soap and heat to create a non-woven fabric (see page 26).

WOOL BATT A quantity of wool taken off the carding drums in sheet form, with misaligned fibre arrangement preserved, aiding the felting process.

Acknowledgements

Grandpa Charlie and multi-award-winning Five Oaks Mabel The Twentieth.

For the Charlies in my life: Grandpa Charlie and his
love of farming; my Charlie and his persistent honesty.

For my family. Make no bones about it, they would rather I were
an academic, but they are always gracious in their disappointment.

Thanks to Jane Graham Maw, my book agent, for the clarity.
With thanks to everyone at Jacqui Small, particularly my editor,
Zia Mattocks, for the longest phone calls ever, and your patience.
And Brent Darby, your photographs are lovely. It was a pleasure.

ABOUT THE AUTHOR

Fi Oberon has 30 years' experience as a designer, maker and workshop tutor.
She prides herself on her originality, inventing new techniques and designs that
enable more people to enjoy their innate creativity. Fi has designed and delivered
many unique projects over the course of her career. At the age of 18 she sold her
first knitting pattern to a Fleet Street newspaper, and since then her work has been
featured in a multitude of national magazines.

In 2006 Fi sold her successful Cotswolds-based Craft Centre to raise her
child by the sea, where she opened a small seasonal art and craft gallery.
Her felting and fine artwork is displayed at galleries in the Midlands and the
north of England, including the prestigious Dean Clough Galleries in Halifax.
In 2014 she launched a range of felting kits and greetings cards featuring
needle-felted animals, and in 2016 she launched her Holiday Craft Box scheme
through selected galleries. Fi runs workshops at national events, including The
Knitting and Stitching Shows and Country Living Fairs. This is her first book.